Repairing
Your MRP System

Shaun
Snapp

Contents

CHAPTER 1

Introduction

MRP stands for "materials requirements planning."

"Material requirements planning software (MRP) is used to describe the process of planning manufacturing inventory – what products to make and what items to buy, when, how much, and from who – all based on supply and demand." – What is MRP Software

MRP is one of the most important methods in supply chain planning. In performing research for this book, I found that MRP is the most commonly used term in supply chain planning, the next closest one being inventory management. This is true even though MRP is an old planning method, and more advanced methods of creating the initial supply and production plan have been created. However, MRP, and its cousin DRP (MRP used for bringing material into the supply network, while DRP pushes material through the supply network), while old, are still the most common methods of performing supply, production and deployment planning. Interestingly, MRP is a much more commonly used term than DRP, or distribution resource planning, which is almost always used in conjunction with MRP and is the other topic covered in this book. In most instances, when a company talks about their MRP system, they actually mean their MRP/DRP system. But while both methods are used, I will be focusing on MRP for this book.

MRP is a procedure for **calculating dependent requirements** based upon a bill of materials working backwards from the demand (also called "independent requirements") of a forecasted item (MRP is emphatically a forecast-based planning method) along with sales orders which, when combined with lead times, creates a series of planned production orders and purchase requisitions which are all timed to allow the demand to be met with the planned supply. MRP has these frequently unstated prerequisites:

1. Every inventory item moves into and out of stock.

2. All components of an assembly are required at the time the assembly order is released.

3. Components are disbursed and used in discrete lots.

4. *Each manufacturing item can be processed independently of any other.* - Orlicky's Material Requirements Planning.

MRP was developed in the 1960's in the US, and incorporated into software and rolled out to companies on a small scale in the 1970's in most of the developed countries, becoming a dominant method of supply and production planning in the 1980's. Reorder point planning was incorporated into software roughly 10 years prior to MRP applications being sold and used, but given the immaturity of computer systems in the 1960's, few companies actually used these reorder point systems. Therefore, there was no significant period of computerized re-order point systems prior to MRP systems. MRP can be considered to be the first broadly used computerized procedure for supply and production planning.

As will be explained in this book, the actual full leveraging of MRP's capabilities change depending upon the company, with some companies still having problems properly using MRP, and with many companies applying MRP incorrectly to unforecastable product locations. This brings up the topic of forecastability and unforecastability, which is a primary determining factor in what supply planning method should be used for a particular product/location combination. This concept of forecastability is discussed in Chapter 8: Specific Steps for Improving MRP.

How is MRP Categorized within Planning?

MRP is one method of creating the **initial** supply plan. For instance, SAP calls this planning run the **location or network planning run** in their advanced planning product (this is in the Supply Network Planning Heuristic, which roughly approximates MRP) .

Notice the two options, to either run the SNP Heuristic in the Network or the Location mode.

Unfortunately there is no standard term used to describe the run. MRP plans procurement and production, but not deployment – which comes after this run and is performed in DRP. The first supply planning run that is part of the normal planning flow I call the "initial" supply planning run. A complete supply planning solution always has at least two planning components (but there are always more than this, examples of which will be provided shortly). The first is the planning of production orders and purchase requisitions to bring into facilities. This brings material into the supply network and schedules production (more detailed production planning often is performed further on in the workflow by a specialized production planning application). The second component is the deployment plan where planned stock transfers are created to push material between the internal locations and finally out to wholesale or retail locations. I could make the argument that there should also be a third component called redeployment, where stock is repositioned periodically between the internal locations, but that takes us into a tangential area and most companies do not use redeployment applications, although I could argue that many more should. Redeployment is not simply a slight tweak to deployment logic, but is an entirely different set of logic, which is why companies often get into trouble when trying to use deployment logic/functionality in supply planning applications for redeployment. Redeployment is explained at the following link:

http://www.scmfocus.com/inventoryoptimizationmultiechelon/2011/10/redeployment/

The Methods Available for Supply Planning

Before we get into how to use multiple supply planning methods, let's review the supply planning methods that are available. Now is also a good time to explain that this book covers multiple methods for either the S&OP and rough-cut capacity plan or the initial supply plan, but does not cover using multiple methods for the deployment plan or for the redeployment. There is a reason for this: while S&OP, rough-cut capacity plan and the initial supply plan use the same methods, only in rare instances would the deployment and redeployment plan use multiple methods. A brief explanation of the different supply planning threads is included below:

1. *S&OP & Rough-Cut Capacity Plan:* Long-range planning threads that are generally not part of the live environment. Used for analytical pur-

poses rather than to drive recommendations to the ERP system. MRP can provide some of the information required for these plans.

2. *The Initial Supply Plan (performed by MRP in ERP systems):* Produces initial production and procurement plan.[1] Focused on bringing stock into the supply network, and in creating stock with planned production orders. Can also be called the master production schedule (MPS), if the initial supply plan is run under certain criteria.

   http://www.scmfocus.com/supplyplanning/2011/10/02/the-four-factors-that-make-up-the-master-production-schedule/

3. *The Deployment Plan (performed by DRP in ERP systems):* Focused on pushing stock from locations at the beginning of the supply network to the end of the supply network.

4. *The Redeployment Plan (performed by specialized applications with redeployment functionality or with a custom report):* Focused on repositioning stock, which is already in the supply network to locations where it has a higher probability of consumption.

---

[1] By creating planned production orders, MRP creates the initial production plan. Through the second step of capacity leveling, an MRP system can create a leveled production plan. However, MRP should not be considered, and not be used, as the main production planning system. By creating a supply plan and production plan together, MRP – as with most other supply planning methods - synchronizes the supply and production plan. But this is not the final production plan. The final production plan should be created by a specific production planning application, which has far more capabilities in this area than any MRP system. The MRP system (or other supply planning system) is then updated with the results of the planning run from the production planning system.

Secondly, that is not the end of the story because there is then the step of creating the production schedule. The production schedule brings the plan down to the hour and minute. Hence the phrase "detailed scheduling." This provides the specifics that are required to manage a factory at maximum efficiency – and with the lowest waste and highest throughput. However, many companies do also rely upon their MRP system for both production planning and partially for production scheduling – although it is essentially impossible to perform detailed scheduling in MRP systems, so companies typically combine the use of MRP with Excel. This is a fair representation of what happens, but companies that operate this way leave throughput "on the table" unless they have the simplest scheduling environments.

Sufficed to say, all supply planning methods must be able to create both an initial supply plan and the deployment plan, or must be able to perform one or the other.

The Complexity of Method Combination

The tricky part is in understanding how to logically combine the different methods into a coherent solution. Much time is spent debating among the different supply planning methods, but very little is written on how to properly integrate multiple methods. That is unfortunate because all methods and method modifiers can be of value in some circumstances. Furthermore, the various supply planning methods cannot not be compared simply on the basis of their sophistication, which is the most common way to grade each method. Some methods are extremely sophisticated, but are also complex, expensive and challenging to implement, to troubleshoot and to explain. For instance, the most complex methods in supply planning are optimization (both cost based and inventory optimization and multi-echelon planning). These methods can provide superior output if implemented correctly, but they cost quite a bit more to implement.

There are debates as to which methods have the highest maintenance costs, because maintenance must be segmented into the costs associated with the planners (or the business side of maintenance) versus the IT costs of maintaining the solution. For example, most companies that implemented advanced supply planning applications since the mid-1990's are, in fact, still using MRP and DRP. While these applications are inexpensive to maintain from an IT perspective (relatively speaking), they require more maintenance by planners who must make adjustments to the results.

Because this topic is complex and multifaceted, I will halt the coverage here. It is, however, a primary topic of the SCM Focus Press book, *Supply Planning with MRP, DRP and APS Software*. A complex supply planning method may be a perfect fit for a company; the company may implement it quite well. However, a complex supply planning method may take too much processing time for every product location in the entire supply network; but moving some product locations that do not require the complexity of the solution to a simpler method may reduce the run time of the planning run, making the overall solution feasible.

When MRP systems were first introduced, DRP had not yet been invented, so reorder point planning was used to trigger deployment.

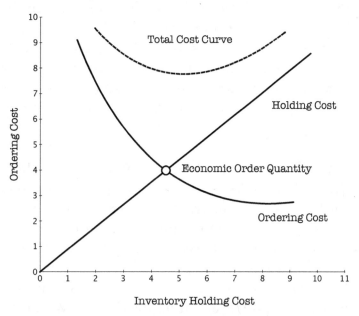

Reorder points are probably the easiest planning method to understand. They are often based upon an economic order quantity, which determines the batch size (or instead can be based upon the minimum order quantity). From there, reorder point is calculated, which accounts for the typical demand as well as the average lead time.[2]

Reorder points were commonly used for the deployment. Different methods can be used for the initial supply plan and the deployment plan. There is no rule saying that, for instance, if a company chooses MRP for the initial supply planning run that it must use DRP for the deployment planning run. However, many systems only have MRP and DRP to work with. Therefore the combination of MRP and DRP for all of a company's supply and production planning needs is the most common combination currently in use.

---

[2] A very easy to use and convenient dynamic reorder point calculator is available at the following link:
http://www.scmfocus.com/supplyplanning/2014/04/09/dynamic-reorder-point-calculator/

What About the Initial Production Plan?

MRP is a supply planning method, however, it also creates the initial production plan, as it assigns planned production orders to days for internally produced product. This led one of my previous clients to state that *"supply planning and production planning are the same thing."* This is actually not true, but it is true that many of the methods used for supply planning are also used for production planning (being quite different from production scheduling). However, on the other hand, not all supply planning methods are also used for production planning. For example, the method called inventory optimization and multi-echelon planning simply creates undifferentiated (between production and procurement) requisitions, which the system then asks the ERP system to sort out.

How the Term MRP is Often Over-used and Misused

MRP, along with the terms "MPS" or "master production schedule" and the term "optimization", are some of the most over-used and misused terms in supply chain planning. MRP is commonplace and so widely used that people in companies often fall into the trap of comingling the term MRP with the process it is performing - either supply planning, production planning, BOM explosion or lead time calculation. However, MRP is a distinct method or procedure that has specific logic and is applied by an application, with the process it is performing. Therefore, I will often find on projects that the term MRP persists even when a different planning method is used. The issue is that MRP is often a proxy for the term "initial supply plan" or "initial production plan." This is a problem because incorrect terminology interferes with companies properly understanding what the procedures are in the system that they are using. Also if you actually don't know the difference between how an MRP run operates and an initial supply plan created by say a cost optimizer, you are less likely to have success implementing your optimizer application for supply planning. While it is often used to mean the initial supply and initial production plan by any method, in fact MRP is a specific method. **It is not, and was never meant to be, a generic term to describe a process**. MRP is one of five methods for creating the initial supply and production plan, the others being the following:

1. Heuristics

2. Allocation or Prioritization

3. Cost Optimization

4. Inventory Optimization Multi-Echelon Planning

Books and Other Publications on MRP

As with all my books, I performed a comprehensive literature review before I began writing. One of my favorite quotations about research is from the highly respected RAND Corporation, a "think tank" based in sunny Santa Monica, CA. They are located not far from where I grew up. On my lost surfing weekends during high school, I used to walk right by their offices with my friend - at that time having no idea of the institution's historical significance. RAND's *Standards for High Quality Research and Analysis* publication makes the following statement about how its research references other work.

> *"A high-quality study cannot be done in intellectual isolation:*
> *It necessarily builds on and contributes to a body of research*
> *and analysis. The relationships between a given study and*
> *its predecessors should be rich and explicit. The study team's*
> *understanding of past research should be evident in many aspects*
> *of its work, from the way in which the problem is formulated and*
> *approached to the discussion of the findings and their implications.*
> *The team should take particular care to explain the ways in which*
> *its study agrees, disagrees, or otherwise differs importantly from*
> *previous studies. Failure to demonstrate an understanding of*
> *previous research lowers the perceived quality of a study, despite any*
> *other good characteristics it may possess."*

There are several books already on MRP, including my previous book *Supply Planning with MRP, DRP and APS Software*. I want to differentiate these MRP books from books on MRP II. MRP II is actually not MRP, but is now a dated term which roughly translates to the term ERP. So if we stick to strictly MRP books, considering how important MRP is to so many companies there are not really that many books on the topic. Having read these books, I would say the book you are reading book is differentiated in the following important ways:

1. *Improvement Oriented:* It is focused on improving the common problems with MRP systems.

2. *Software Focus*: This book will cover MRP conceptually, but this book is primarily about getting MRP **software** to work better.

3. *Experience Level*: This book is towards the advanced end of the spectrum. It assumes a basic knowledge of MRP.

4. *Non-Promotional*: Many books on a method like MRP are focused on promoting MRP versus other methods. This book does not do that. MRP has advantages and disadvantages over comparative methods, but this book does not spend time trying to convince companies to use any one particular method. For an overall comparison of each of the supply and production planning methods, my other book, *MRP and DRP, Supply Planning with MRP, DRP and APS Software*.

The Use of Screen Shots in the Book

I consult in some popular and well-known applications, and I've found that companies have often been given the wrong impression of an application's capabilities. As part of my consulting work, I am required to present the results of testing and research about various applications. The research may show that a well-known application is not able to perform some functionality well enough to be used by a company, and points to a lesser-known application where this functionality is easily performed. Because I am routinely in this situation, I am asked to provide evidence of the testing results within applications, and screen shots provide this necessary evidence.

Furthermore, some time ago, it became a habit for me to include extensive screen shots in most of my project documentation. A screen shot does not, of course, guarantee that a particular functionality works, but it is the best that can be done in a document format. Everything in this book exists in one application or another, and nothing described in this book is hypothetical.

Timing Field Definitions Identification

This book is filled with lists. Some of these lists are field definitions. The way to quickly identify which lists are field definitions is that they will be all *italics*, while lists that are not field definitions will be only *italics* for the term defined, while the definition that follows is not in normal text.

How Writing Bias Is Controlled at SCM Focus and SCM Focus Press

Bias is a serious problem in the enterprise software field. Large vendors receive uncritical coverage of their products, and large consulting companies recommend the large vendors that have the resources to hire and pay consultants rather than the vendors with the best software for the client's needs.

At SCM Focus, we have yet to financially benefit from a company's decision to buy an application showcased in print, either in a book or on the SCM Focus website. This may change in the future as SCM Focus grows – but we have been writing with a strong viewpoint for years without coming into any conflicts of interest. SCM Focus has the most stringent rules related to controlling bias and restricting commercial influence of any information provider. These "writing rules" are provided in the link below:

http://www.scmfocus.com/writing-rules/

If other information providers followed these rules, we would be able to learn about software without being required to perform our own research and testing for every topic.

Information about enterprise supply chain planning software can be found on the internet, but this information is primarily promotional or written at such a high level that none of the important details or limitations of the application are exposed; this is true of books as well. When only one enterprise software application is covered in a book, one will find that the application works perfectly, the application operates as expected and there are no problems during the implementation to bring the application live. This is all quite amazing and quite different from my experience of implementing enterprise software. However, it is very difficult to make a living by providing objective information about enterprise supply chain software, especially as it means being critical at some point. I once remarked to a friend that SCM Focus had very little competition in providing untarnished information on this software category, and he said, "Of course, there is no money in it."

The Approach to the Book

By writing this book, I wanted to help people get exactly the information they need without having to read a lengthy volume. The approach to the book is essentially the same as to my previous books, and in writing this book I followed the same principles.

1. **Be direct and concise.** There is very little theory in this book and the math that I cover is simple. While the mathematics behind the optimization methods for supply and production planning is involved, there are plenty of books which cover this topic. This book is focused on software and for most users and implementers of the software the most important thing to understand is conceptually what the software is doing.

2. **Based on project experience.** Nothing in the book is hypothetical; I have worked with it or tested it on an actual project. My project experience has led to my understanding a number of things that are not covered in typical supply planning books. In this book, I pass on this understanding to you.

3. **Saturate the book with graphics.** Roughly two-thirds of a human's sensory input is visual, and books that do not use graphics - especially educational and training books such as this one - can fall short of their purpose. Graphics have also been used consistently and extensively on the SCM Focus website.

The SCM Focus Site

As I am also the author of the SCM Focus site, http://www.scmfocus.com, the site and the book share a number of concepts and graphics. Furthermore, this book contains many links to articles on the site, which provide more detail on specific subjects. This book provides an explanation of how supply and production planning software works and aims to continue to be a reference after its initial reading. However, if your interest in supply planning software continues to grow, the SCM Focus site is a good resource to which articles are continually added.

The SCM site dedicated specifically to supply planning is http://www.scmfocus. com/supplyplanning

Intended Audience

This book is for anyone interested in better understanding MRP. This book covers MRP from a conceptual, a systems and a nuts-and-bolts perspective. Literally anyone who wants to understand how to properly run MRP systems can benefit from this book. If you have any questions or comments on the book, please e-mail me at shaunsnapp@scmfocus.com.

Abbreviations

A listing of all abbreviations used throughout the book is provided at the end of the book.

Corrections

Corrections and updates, as well as reader comments, can be viewed in the comment section of this book's web page. If you have comments or questions, please add them to the following link:

http://www.scmfocus.com/scmfocuspress/supply-books/repairing-mrp-system/

CHAPTER 2

The Opportunity to Improve MRP

I entered the field in 1998 working for an advanced planning software vendor, and the assumption which was generally accepted within this vendor was that MRP had been mastered by companies and that it was time for more advanced methods. This was the philosophy throughout the software vendor, but roughly 17 years of experience in the field later, it seems a completely incorrect assumption. It is well recognized that the way that MRP is implemented and run in most companies leaves a significant opportunity for improvement. This is both the conclusion of many of those who work and have published in this area, as well as my own conclusion – although this type of opportunity actually generalizes to all supply chain planning systems that I have worked with, and to other systems as well. However, the fact that MRP is so prevalent within companies means that the opportunity for improvement exists in most companies. I found these quotations insightful from an early adopter of MRP.

"Our information systems developed into "islands", beginning with accounting, inventory, purchasing, etc., with no overall master plan to guide their interaction. We structured our people around functions, placing them into classes, separated them by walls, and then tried to manage this with MRP.

Most companies that we interface with seldom get through more than 60% of the MRP review reports weekly. Because the extensive amount of variances aren't maintained, over time the effect is usually a build-up of unneeded materials, a consequential rise in inventory, and continued daily anguish over missing parts.

Most companies haven't learned from the high washout rate that MRP has produced. Companies continue to pursue MRP implementations without regard to the real causes of their problems. A survey by Ingersoll Engineers revealed that companies with the least experience in extensive systems implementations are most likely to forge ahead with complex integrated manufacturing support systems such as ERP."

– The Rise and Fall of MRP

The General Knowledge Level of MRP

It is remarkable to me that, at this late date, MRP is often so poorly understood by the people that both work in it but also manage MRP systems. MRP, and by extension DRP (DRP is based upon MRP), is very simple and the fact they are still not properly understood is quite a stinging critique of the ability of companies to train their employees, and organizations like APICS to provide elementary education in supply chain management. However, this criticism extends to universities as well that both offer too few supply chain programs and that do not cover major procedures like MRP. It is difficult to see why every student of supply chain should not have had exposure to an MRP system, or to have the opportunity to actually create and adjust a plan by the time they graduate. However, even if this were to occur, the vast majority of people working in supply chain planning have no formal education in the topics in which they work. Many lack the math confidence to really excel as planners. The question over what degree to teach vocational versus higher-minded topics is a long-running debate. However, there is little doubt that supply chain management continues to be a greatly under-taught topic when compared to other business topics. When one looks at the number of available marketing positions versus the number of available supply chain positions, many more people study marketing that end up in marketing than those that study supply chain and end up in supply chain management. Of course marketing is more glamorous and also tends to pay better. Generally, the more technically advanced people working in supply chain tend to be engineers and are also often not trained in supply chain concepts. The closest area of engineering to supply chain is industrial engineering, although I have frequently worked with electrical or mechanical engineers in my consulting career. A very large area of employment, which has extremely few people who have any educational background in the topic, I would say is about as good evidence that I can provide of a poorly designed educational policy.

Who Manages the Policies of the Supply Chain Systems?

I am sorry to say that many Directors and Vice Presidents have only a cursory knowledge of the MRP systems that they are managing. However, this is not the only problem. If someone were to come to me and ask if person XYZ were a good person to put in control of a planning group and they were to tell me that this person had a good knowledge of the technical aspects of demand planning, supply planning and production planning and further that they were savvy in supply chain software and able to manage people, I would still have another question; and that question would be...

"Do they have the confidence and a demonstrated history of pushing back on bad ideas?"

The reason for this is that they will be repeatedly asked to make decisions to improve short-term metrics, which will completely undermine the planning process. Currently, at many companies across the US, Vice Presidents and Directors in supply chain are interfering with planning decisions and having their planners meet antiquated planning targets, **or reactively flush inventory in order to meet short-term objectives.** If the individual who controls policy in supply planning systems lacks the ability to push back on the constant churn of what are often silly ideas of corporate directives (often promoted by consultants) to do this or that to service levels and inventory levels based upon meeting quarterly results, or the flavor of the month of philosophies, they will not be able to maintain a sustainable system even if they have excellent supply chain system domain expertise. The fact that a rather simple procedure (MRP), which was first developed back in the early 1960s, is still not managed very well is perplexing. Perhaps it is why this is not much discussed, that as a society we don't like observing things we don't do very well. The fact that we have many supply chain Directors and Vice Presidents that still say things like "lets forecast every day to improve working capital," is unfortunate, but we can feel better if we don't focus on it.

The fact is, no organization can move to more advanced methods until they have mastered the methods below them. And, of course, the first step to improving something you are not very good at is admitting that it is a problem.

Background on the Financial Returns of MRP Systems

The SCM Focus Press book *The Real Story Behind ERP: Separating Fact from Fiction*, evaluates the various proposals that were used to sell ERP systems, and in evaluating the research on the financial and operational benefits/ROI of ERP. The results are surprisingly poor to many that now consider ERP to be "critical infrastructure." Part of the value of ERP systems is that they provide MRP and DRP integrated to other ERP functionality. This was a primary reason that MRP/DRP systems primarily stopped being sold as separate products in the mid-1980's.

Upon investigating the research into the benefits/ROI of MRP, it was surprising to find even less research than had been performed for ERP systems. This means that enormous sums of money have been spent in the enterprise software market without buyers or consulting companies **analyzing the research** of how effective these systems were in meeting their stated results.

The most complete study on MRP that I found was performed by Roger G. Schroeder, John C. Anderson, Sharon E. Tupy, and Edna M. White in *A Study of MRP Benefits and Costs*, which was published all the way back in 1981. That would have given the authors roughly 10 years to investigate the results, as MRP was just starting to be implemented in the early 1970's and really began to hit a critical mass of implementations in 1975 – but of course leaves out the following 32 years from 1981 to now.

This study found the following improvements in companies that used MRP.

1. Inventory Turnover Increase: 26%

2. Delivery Lead Time Decrease: 20%

3. Percent of Delivery to Promises Increase: 20%

4. Reduction of the Number of People Working in Expediting: 67%

What this research generally proposes is that MRP had a transformative effect on the companies in its study that implemented MRP systems – what else can one conclude from these changes to the state of the companies that implemented MRP in this sample? What is just as interesting is that these same companies **only** rated the MRP system along a variety of goals ranging from "Improved Customer Satisfaction" to "Better Inventory Control," and the average score was 2.46 out of 4. This is right between the improvements being "Some" and "Much" improved.

The Believability of the Results

I have spent quite a few years working on supply chain planning projects, although moving from the use of periodic inventory recalculations performed by people rather than computer considerably predates my entry into the workforce. However, I can easily imagine that the productivity improvement must have been at least as large as is represented in these truncated study results (obviously the 1981 study was looking backwards from 1981). However, how much any initiative improves performance is dependent upon the level of sophistication of the environment prior to the implementation. For instance, the first printing press which was introduced in 1450 was horribly inefficient by any following standard - with a productivity level which meant that one laborer (either pressman or typesetter) would produce roughly 1/4 of a Bible in a month of work. However it was more efficient than the technology it was replacing, which was copying by hand. Therefore, one must consider that it is more than likely that few of these companies even had computer-based reorder point systems in use – as very few of those systems were sold, primarily because MRP systems supplanted them in the marketplace before they could become popular. This study would have been for companies without computers. A group of studies on MRP is discussed in the book *Factory Physics*.

"First from a macro perspective, American manufacturing inventory turns remained roughly constant throughout the 1970's and 1980's, during and after the MRP crusade. On the other hand, it is obvious that many firms were not using MRP during this period; so it appears that MRP did not revolutionize the efficiency of the entire manufacturing sector, these figures alone do not make a clear statement about MRP's effectiveness as the individual firm level. At the micro level, early surveys of MRP users did not paint a rosy picture either. Booz Allen Hamilton, in a 1980 survey of more than 1,100 firms, reported that much less than 10 percent of American and European companies were able to recoup their investment in an MRP system within 2 years. In a 1982 APICS funded survey of 679 APICS members, only 9.5 percent regarded their companies has being class A users. Fully 60 percent reported their firms as being class C or class D users. To appreciate the significance of these responses, we must not that the respondents in this type of survey were all both APICS members and material managers – people with a strong incentive to see MRP in as good a light as possible!"

If we increase the standard somewhat by asking the question of how well the MRP system is leveraged to provide high quality planning output versus how it could be leveraged, it is clear from my experience, and the experience of others, that the gap is vast. In Chapter 8: "Specific Steps for Improving MRP", I will get into the detail of how to shrink this gap.

CHAPTER 3

Where Supply Planning Fits Within the Supply Plan

To begin, it is important to understand how the supply planning methods covered in this book relate within the overall context of enterprise supply chain software. The following mind map shows this relationship.

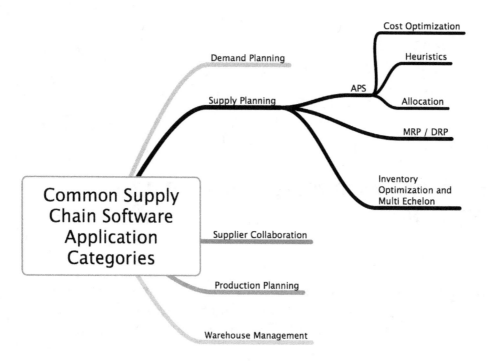

I list supply planning as the second supply chain software category because it immediately follows demand planning as a supply chain planning process. Although demand planning forecasts are used by many processes, including S&OP, the main customer for demand planning forecasts is supply planning. Supplier collaboration integrates with supply planning and uses its planned on-hand stocking data. Product planning also uses data from the supply plan, developing production orders based on the supply plan. Warehouse management indirectly interacts with the supply plan; however, warehouse management systems are more strongly connected to the materials management function of the ERP system than to the supply planning system.

The graphic above does not fully explore the different subcategories within the major categories. For instance, Advanced Planning and Scheduling (APS) solutions also cover demand planning and supplier collaboration, but the purpose of this graphic is to describe APS only as it pertains to supply planning.

As you can see, APS is a catch-all term that describes three different supply planning methods. MRP and DRP are listed together because they are closely related, with DRP essentially being an extension of MRP, but for outbound movements from the factory rather than inbound movements to the factory. MRP and DRP are normally part of the ERP system; however, they can also be located in external planning systems. For instance, SAP APO's PP/DS module has several heuristics that emulate MRP. In another example, Demand Works Smoothie, an external planning system, performs both MRP and DRP.

The Basic Nature of the Supply Chain Planning Functionality in ERP Systems

When I first began working with SAP ERP, I was extremely surprised at the limited functionality that the application contained for supply chain planning. However, what I did not understand at the time was that most deep supply chain capabilities were not the focus of ERP systems. Instead, they put far more development emphasis into things such as finance and accounting, sales order management, and other operational functions, than into supply chain planning. What made these systems popular was their supply chain functionality, which, although basic, was integrated with Finance, HR, etc. And although there have been some improvements since I worked in ERP, advanced supply chain functionality primarily resides outside ERP systems to this day.

How ERP and APS Share the Planning Work

APS and ERP-based MRP work together on projects as a normal method of implementation. The most common approach has been for a company to implement one of the APS methods and then to use MRP in the ERP system to perform the bill of material (BOM) explosion. Under this design, DRP in the ERP system is minimized as it is only used for the deployment of non-critical parts.

Critical versus Non-critical Materials

In MRP, the product database is often segmented into critical and non-critical materials, as described below.

- Critical materials, typically strategic, have longer lead times or are constrained by capacity.

- Non-critical materials are not restricted or difficult to obtain. As such, there is no compelling reason to put very much effort into planning non-critical materials.

After the critical materials have been identified, they are brought over from the ERP system to the external APS system (which resides on different hardware than the ERP system). Under this design, the APS system could apply any of its methods to the critical materials. The following options are possible:

- APS could apply its methods to just the finished goods, while the ERP system would perform all planning for the subcomponents.

- The APS system could apply its methods to both the finished goods and to the subcomponents.

Dependent Demand Products

Secondly, while dependent demand products such as subcomponents may make up a great deal of the products to be planned, they do not necessarily need to be forecasted or have advanced supply planning methods applied to them, as their procurement and deployment is entirely dependent upon the manufactured product and they are simply part of the BOM. Therefore, dependent demand products do not necessarily have to exist in external supply or demand planning systems. The MRP function of "exploding" the BOM and the creation of dependent demand procurement requisitions can occur in the ERP system after all demand and supply planning activities have been performed in external planning systems. The supply planning system then applies the selected method on these critical and independent demand products (those that have demand directly forecasted for them and which have their own BOM). Once the plan is complete, the transaction recommendations (planned purchase orders, planned stock transfer orders, planned repair orders, and planned production orders - all of which can also be called either "planned orders" or "requisitions" as both terms are equally accurate) are sent to the ERP system for execution. To develop dependent requirements for subcomponents and to calculate independent and dependent requirements for non-critical materials that are also not planned in the APS, MRP is run in ERP, which explodes the BOM (extensively covered in the SCM Focus Press book *Supply Planning with MRP/ DRP and APS Software*, while BOM explosion is covered in Chapter 5: "MRP Explained"). If non-critical products are kept outside of the external planning system, as per the design above, then DRP is necessary in the ERP system to move these non-critical products, as they have not been planned in the APS system through the supply network.

This is commonly how MRP and DRP (supply planning methods that reside in one system: ERP) interact with the APS supply planning methods (heuristics, allocation, cost optimization), which are applied against products in another system.

Alternative Design

However, the design described above is not the only design. A second design plans both critical and non-critical products in the APS system, but not subcomponents. Under this design, MRP is still used to explode the BOM and create order requisitions for subcomponent procurement, but DRP is not required because the deployment of the non-critical products is managed by the external planning system. An additional point is that MRP is not the only mechanism within most ERP systems to perform BOM explosion. For instance in SAP ERP, the XO MRP Type's definition is "W/O MRP, with BOM Explosion." Therefore, while MRP is the most common way of exploding the BOM in ERP systems, it is not the only method available.

A third design is to plan all critical and non-critical products and subcomponents in the APS system and then to send the transaction recommendations over to the ERP system to perform execution only. In this case, neither MRP nor DRP is required to be run in the ERP system because all the planning for all the products and all subcomponents has already been performed in the APS system. Specifically, the BOM has already been exploded, and the subcomponent (dependent demand) procurement recommendations and the deployment plan/stock transport requisitions for non-critical products have already been created.

Where a Product/Location Combination is "Planned"

Some of the examples above demonstrate why it's important to add more specifics to the term "planned." Unfortunately it is very easy to fall into the habit of saying that a product is planned in one system or another, when in fact we generally speak of a product being planned in one system only. For instance, the most common distinction is the one made above where critical products are *planned entirely* in the SAP APO application versus non-critical products being *planned entirely* (usually with MRP) in the ERP system. Under this design, the delineation between being "planned" in one system or another is very clear. However, this distinction becomes less clear when one of the planning stages is performed in one system and a second in another. This is because "planned in" is not a sufficiently detailed description to explain what is happening and where it is happening. A product can have the finished good planning performed in APO, with the subcomponents planned either with MRP or with simple BOM explosion. For products with multiple nesting in their bill of material, the finished good could be planned in APO, with the semi-finished good and raw material planned in R/3. Alternatively, both the finished good and semi-finished good could be planned in APO, and only the raw material planned in R/3.

Conclusion

Supply planning software sits between demand planning and applications such as supplier collaboration and production planning. It is often considered the intersection point or heart of the supply chain planning process, because it interacts with all the other major planning components. Supply planning systems can perform first-cut production planning by incorporating production batch sizes and production capacity constraints into the supply planning system.

All supply planning is performed by no more than six methods (the sixth being inventory optimization and multi-echelon planning) by all companies globally. However, because MRP is not a complete supply planning method without DRP, the methods can be counted in two different ways. Therefore I often combine MRP/DRP into one method, which would make for only five methods. In order for a method to be complete, it must address both the initial plan and the deployment plan. The initial plan (or network plan as it is sometimes called) is the production and procurement plan, while the deployment plan creates stock transfer recommendations between the supply network locations. All the other methods (not MRP and DRP) can be used for either the initial supply plan or for the deployment plan. However, they do so with different parameters in place. Therefore, the configuration for cost optimization or allocation (often stored in some type of profile) for deployment is a completely separate configuration from the allocation or cost optimization that controls the initial or network plan. MRP and DRP are the only methods that perform "one half" of the supply planning process only. Therefore while they are broadly known as two different things, they can be thought of as complementary parts of one method.

MRP/DRP is normally run from an ERP system but it can also be performed in APS systems. One supply planning application called Demand Works Smoothie performs MRP/DRP but is neither an APS system nor an ERP system. APS supply planning methods are usually co-implemented with MRP/DRP functionality in order to develop a supply plan for both critical and non-critical materials, and three different designs for accomplishing this have been listed and are generally well known. Most likely more designs exist, as it is difficult to guess all the ways that companies have decided to connect their external supply planning systems to their ERP systems.

CHAPTER 4

MRP Versus MRP II

MRP was a term and technology that arose in the 1970's, while MRP II was a term and technology or more accurately a group of technologies that arose in the 1980's. MRP II sounds identical as if it is just some type of enhancement over MRP, but the acronym of MRP II does not stand for the same thing as MRP. MRP II stands for "manufacturing resource planning." While MRP is **contained within MRP II**, they are not at all the same thing, and in fact this is a common area of confusion. It is very important when discussing MRP that we ensure that we are all talking about the same thing. I did not plan to cover anything but MRP in this book and, for reasons that will be explained, the term MRP II existed during a particular time before another term supplanted it. I never use the term MRP II in my consulting work, but it does come up because there is still a residue of exposure to MRP II on projects. **In fact, there are more books on the topic of MRP II than there are on the topic of MRP.** But this seems to have little effect except to confuse the discussion of MRP. In this chapter we will unravel the history and differences between MRP and MRP II. Lets begin by covering MRP II.

What is MRP II?

Oliver Wight popularized MRP II. Oliver Wight was already well-established in MRP decades before developing MRP II and is a co-author, often with another MRP, as well as overall production planning and inventory management guru, George Plossl.

MRP II is well described a category of software. At first there was stand-alone MRP software. However, as time passed, software vendors began adding extra functionality that, while connected to MRP, was not actually part of MRP. The graphic below explains the net change from MRP to MRP II as well as the net change between MRP II and ERP. The idea was that a term had to be created to describe systems that became much more than simply MRP.

ERP =
MRP II + Sales + Finance

MRP II =
MRP + Production Scheduling + Capacity Leveling

MRP =
1. BOM explosion
2. Order date calculation based upon lead times
3. Automated order sizing & inventory control through parameters

As can be seen above, MRP II was actually an intermediate stage between MRP and ERP. However, with the takeover of ERP systems by the late 1980's, software companies stopped selling their software as MRP II software, although the concept of MRP II is still sometimes discussed.

As with most ideas that become popular in supply chain management, what something is, is a combination of its actual features with how the item is expressed, which often has a lot to do with marketing. If we draw a distinction between MRP II as a system and MRP II as a concept, it is clear that MRP II as a concept was originally introduced based upon the marketing platform that MRP had not achieved its objectives. The argument went that this was **because MRP was insufficiently integrated** into the rest of the business and lacked some specific functionalities. The quotation below explains this idea.

> *"By far, the greatest single factor in ruining a perfectly good manufacturing plan is the tendency for the Demand Forecast to change on a regular basis, **typically inside planning lead time.** Or, the Demand Forecast may be completely useless for manufacturing purposes, forcing the person responsible for the master schedule to literally generate his own forecast in an attempt to predict what the demand actually will be. Often times, a combination of both of these conditions exists, where the marketing forecast is so inaccurate as to make it useless, forcing the master scheduler to perform this task of generating a forecast. And, without some kind of forecast, there is **no master schedule**. And, without a master schedule, there is no 'M.R.P.'. Any 'M.R.P.' system without a demand forecast analysis capability is thus severely limited in its ability to help reduce overall inventory and simultaneously meet the requirements of the production plan. After all, "Garbage In, Garbage Out."*
>
> – What is MRP (I,II)

I want to be clear that I don't use this quotation because I agree with it, but because it illustrates the arguments presented for MRP II at the time. The issues with MRP then and now are not primarily because of a lack of integration – but the concept of improving systems, not through enhancing functionality but through integration to other functionality, has been a very effective marketing theme for software vendors. The constant emphasis on integration has caused a complete overestimation of the actual integration costs of connecting systems on the part of executive decision makers in the software buyers.[1] Interestingly, 30 years after the introduction of MRP II, this problem persists. For instance, connecting a low accuracy forecast to an MRP system through an integrated system does nothing of benefit because MRP is a forecast-based system. How to deal with high forecast error product/location combination is covered in Chapter 7: "When MRP is Applicable."

The Focus of MRP II

MRP II, while sounding almost exactly like MRP, is in fact **not** focused on the same things as MRP. MRP II more or less simply accepts MRP as a supporting capability - which is then extended with MRP II.

Instead MRP II is focused on the integration between MRP and the **new functionalities of capacity planning and detailed scheduling**. MRP II as a concept, rather than the MRP II system, is also more qualitative than MRP and more focused on process. For instance, Oliver Wight began a consulting company that certified companies in MRP II. In his 1983 book, the following are examples of the checklist criteria used by Oliver Wight Consulting to certify a company in *Class A for Business Excellence.*

1. *Understanding and Analyzing the Internal and External Environment:* A process exists to collect relevant information internally and externally to understand the company, its products and services, its market place and the competition.

2. *Company Capability:* The company has a business process to understand the capability of all its business processes to identify the strengths and

---

[1] Estimations at Software Decisions, the paid research sub site within SCM Focus, estimates integration costs for a variety of enterprise applications within 10 categories of software. From this research it is clear that integration costs should never drive the decision of what software to purchase. The most important consideration in software selection is the match between the business requirements and the functionality of the application. This research is available at http://www.softwaredecisions.org. A full explanation of the areas of software to focus on for effective software selections, as well as how to cut through the clutter of financially-biased advisors and IT analysts is covered in the SCM Focus Press book *Enterprise Software Selection: How to Pinpoint the Perfect Software Solution using Multiple Source of Information.* http://www.scmfocus.com/scm-focus/it-decision-making-books/enterprise-software-selection/

weaknesses of its offer to the marketplace.

3. *Analytical Tools:* A comprehensive use of analytical tools is made to identify business trends and opportunities and to understand how the company responds to current and future needs.

4. *Vision Statement:* The vision statement is inspiring and memorable and summarizes concisely what the company wants to become in the market place and community.

5. *Supplier Quality:* Supplier quality processes and improvement programs are monitored and reported, to ensure integration with the company's quality systems.

As should be apparent, none of these criteria have anything to do with setting up MRP systems. Other reading of this book shows the overall process rather than the calculation orientation of MRP II. It is difficult to say exactly how effective these types of certifications were, but it is amusing to find this quote from George Plossl, who was a friend and co-author of Oliver Wight, regarding what was the certification program at the time:

> *"Implementation (of MRP) was viewed as "getting software running on the computer" not as using the programs to run the business, so users were poorly prepared, incomplete systems were installed, and proper foundations were not put into place. Under qualified consultants aggravated this by offering to help install MRP II systems and reach in very short time "Class A status," a set of superficial and systems related criteria more than operations-related requirements. Interestingly, there must have been a number of consulting companies offering this Class A status at the time - however, Oliver Wight's checklist do not focus on systems related criteria and are more focused on higher level types of criteria."*

This issue persists to this day in supply chain software implementations and is what I refer to as an IT-centric implementation. All of this is why it's more misleading than clarifying to speak of MRP II in the same sense as MRP. For instance, ERP contains MRP; however, one could never use the terms ERP and MRP interchangeably - but this is often done with MRP and MRP II. While this is not generally understood, this observation was made by George Plossl all the way back in 1984:

> *"Practically all suppliers of MRP programs provide a comprehensive core-system package for manufacturing planning and control, including MRP, rough-cut capacity planning and capacity and shop floor control, plus many support programs for procurement design and process engineering, quality management, cost accounting and plant maintenance. Unfortunately, these are usually called "MRP II systems," leading to confusion between MRP technique and the MRP system they represent. Sophistication of programming of these systems is also overdone.*
>
> *"The acronym (MRP II) was an unfortunate choice, causing confusion and generating more heat than light on he subject of improving operations."*

Plossel points out the confusing aspects of calling all these functions "MRP II" (shortly after, this same set of functionalities would be called ERP, a term coined by Gartner), but Plossl also makes the point about the sophistication of the **programming being overdone** –which, if you read other quotations by him, and which I cover in a separate article, is that this over-sophistication negatively impacts the implementability of these (what are now referred to as ERP) applications. This is not a quote from 5 or 10 years ago, but from 30 years ago.

Conclusion

A way to begin this chapter was by drawing a distinction between MRP and MRP II. This was necessary because the concept of MRP II, while related, has muddied the waters on discussions and on the understanding of MRP. There are still some companies where the term and vocabulary as well as the much larger scope of MRP II is confused with the scope of MRP. MRP II was introduced with a great deal of fanfare, and in fact there are more books on MRP II than MRP; however, its actual impact is far smaller than MRP, unless one translates MRP II into ERP systems, but in that case we are talking about a great deal more than supply and production planning. In most cases, MRP II is far more confusing than actually helpful, and the point of this chapter was to have the reader put aside concepts of MRP II when we discuss MRP.

CHAPTER 5

MRP Explained

Materials Requirements Planning, or MRP, was the first supply planning method to be computerized. MRP can create purchase requisitions and initial production requisitions. However, MRP does not have the information necessary to schedule production and is not aware of production constraints. For this reason, I like to call MRP a method for "initial" planning only and production requisitions created by MRP should be considered a first pass. These production requisitions are really just translations of demand quantities and dates adjusted for lead times. Either they must be capacity-leveled in the ERP system, or sent to a production planning and scheduling system.

A Brief History of MRP

MRP's initial focus was not material requirements planning. MRP first stood for "manufacturing requirements planning" before it was renamed to "materials requirements planning". Unlike the planning methods that were being researched at the time and were implemented after MRP, MRP was not developed by academics. Instead, it was developed by practitioners in the field. While roughly a decade passed after MRP's development before a substantial number of companies began to use it, the timeframe is actually remarkably fast for a new supply planning method.

Prior to MRP, reorder point methods and manual methods drove the planning. Back then, many of the calculations had to be performed by hand because computational and data storage capabilities limited the types of planning mathematics and techniques that could be used. Interestingly, there are papers on multi-echelon that date from the late 1950's and papers for inventory optimization from the mid-1970's. Nonetheless it was decades before inventory optimization mathematics could be actually implemented in enterprise software. MRP on the other hand, was much faster out of the gate.

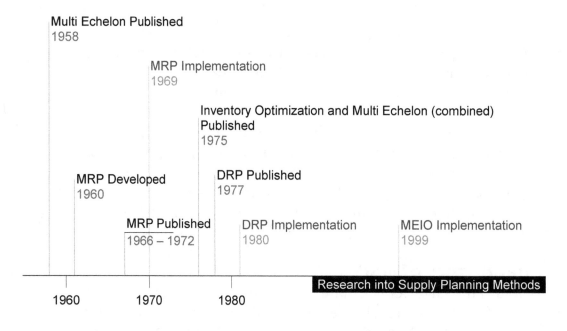

The lag time between development and commercialization and general implementation for simpler methods of supply planning (MRP and DRP) was much shorter than for more advanced methods. Research into advanced methods like multi-echelon planning actually <u>preceded</u> MRP by several years, but while MRP started to be broadly implemented within 10 years of its initial development, it would be 40 years after multi-echelon's initial development before it would be used in commercial applications.

Only recently have many of the hardware constraints mentioned previously been lifted, although more and more options become available with every passing year. Reorder point methods are still used to control procurement and sometimes production; however, they now work with MRP to create economic order quantities. (They can also be used without MRP and are covered in detail in the SCM Focus Press book *Supply Planning with MRP, DRP and APS Software.*) Even though MRP is mathematically simple, it performs a number of repetitive calculations that prior to MRP had to be calculated manually, which was a tedious task. Converting large volumes of sales orders into production orders and purchase orders was quite a feat when this capability was first developed independently in the early 1960's at J. I. CASE and Stanley Tools. Yet quite a few companies continued using their old systems before industry converted over to MRP in the late 1970's.

What MRP Includes

The easiest way to understand MRP is to understand what is included in the MRP calculation that generates production and procurement orders:

- Sales Orders

- Purchase Orders

- Materials

- Stock (There are many different types of stock, but only unrestricted and valuated stock can be included in MRP. In addition, while optional, MRP should be set to incorporate the stock in transit.)

- Material Lead Times

- Components

- Assemblies

- Lot Size

- Resources/Work Centers

What MRP Does Not Include

MRP is very simple; it has fewer options and configuration requirements when compared to the other methods for performing initial planning (production and procurement planning). Therefore, it is also useful to understand what MRP does not include.

- *Normal Stock Transfers*: Notice that unlike APS or DRP, MRP does not create stock transfers. This is because it has no concept of the relationships between facilities and is not a method for deployment.

- *Inventory Balancing Stock Transfers*: MRP does not rebalance inventory to meet future demand the way several supply planning methods do.

- *Prioritization:* MRP does not understand priority; it only understands quantities, dates and lead times. Consequently, if a high-priority customer places an order for product later than a low-priority customer, the low-priority customer receives the inventory. However, many companies operate based on customer priority in addition to the need date, so this is where inventory is either manually allocated or allocation software comes into the equation.

- *Constraints:* One of the great limitations of MRP - and one of the main reasons that constraint-based planning was developed and flourished in the late 1990's - is that it does not know what is feasible; rather it works backwards from requirements and simply develops a plan based upon this figure.

A screenshot of the MRP setup in SAP ERP demonstrates MRP's simplicity and how few options require configuration.

Single-Item, Single-Level

Material	SCM Focus Mat
MRP Area	3800
Plant	AC00

MRP control parameters

Processing key	NETCH	Net change for total horizon
Create purchase req.	2	Purchase requisitions in opening period
Delivery schedules	3	Schedule lines
Create MRP list	1	MRP list
Planning mode	1	Adapt planning data (normal mode)
Scheduling	1	Basic dates will be determined for plann
Planning date	27.03.2012	

Process control parameters

☐ Display results before they are saved

- The first option is the processing key, which relates to whether MRP will reprocess everything (called regenerative planning) or whether it will just perform a net change.

- The second option relates to whether purchase requisitions are within the planning horizon. If purchase requisitions are not created by the system, they can be created manually. One option here allows only planned orders to be created outside the planning horizon.

- The delivery schedule setting controls if and how schedule lines will be created.

- The next setting relates to whether or not an MRP List should be created. The MRP List is the list of the MRP output per material.

- The planning mode setting controls whether the system re-explodes the BOM after each run. This is performed when the BOM for the assembly has changed, and/or the quantity or date of the procurement proposal has changed.

- The scheduling setting controls how dates are determined for planned orders and whether only a basic method will be used to determine the dates of planned orders or whether a more complex method involving lead time scheduling and capacity planning will be used.

As you can see, the options are limited and several are related to such things as reprocessing all orders, determining when to create procurement orders, etc. By contrast, the SNP Supply Network Planning Network Heuristic ,which is a supply and production planning method in the SAP SNP module in APO, and which essentially emulates MRP, has many more controls, including something called "Low Level Codes," which controls the sequence in which the product/location combinations are run. This is described in detail below:

http://www.scmfocus.com/sapplanning/2011/02/04/level-of-bom-planning-in-the-snp-heuristic-and-low-level-codes/

Many companies rely upon SAP ERP to run their MRP, and SAP has a good description of the mechanics of MRP:

> *"The system calculates net requirements for all the requirement quantities that are to be planned. The system thereby compares available warehouse stock or the scheduled receipts from purchasing and production with planned independent requirements, material reservations and incoming sales orders. In the case of a material shortage, that is, if the available stock (including firmed receipts) is smaller than the quantity required, the system creates procurement proposals."*
>
> – SAP MRP Uses and Their Implications

Major Functionality of MRP

Understanding MRP is a great place to start for understanding the other supply planning methods. The major functionality in MRP is shown in the graphic below.

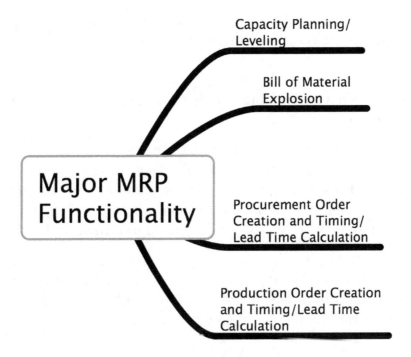

MRP covers the functions listed above. MRP's functionality is basic arithmetic; however, it does so for many products at once and can be rerun quickly compared to other supply planning methods.

Manufacturing Capacity Leveling/Planning

As this book focuses on supply planning, I will not spend much time on the manufacturing side of MRP. However, it is important to know that it exists and the implications it has for the supply plan.

Capacity leveling/planning is the activity of spreading or moving production orders from periods where there is no capacity to periods where there is capacity.[1] Capacity leveling can be carried out with all of the supply planning methods described in this book. Even when capacities are constrained (such as with

---

[1] When capacity leveling is added to MRP, this can be referred to as MRP II. A number of books draw a distinction between MRP and MRP II, however I don't see the term MRP II used in industry, and MRP II involves several other components such as reporting. I don't find MRP II to be a useful concept, so I don't cover it in this book.

cost optimization and allocation), it is often still necessary to perform manual capacity leveling as the resource master data is never 100% accurate.

When infinite capacity planning is configured, capacity leveling is frequently performed with a capacity leveling heuristic. Capacity leveling heuristics have the following limitations:

- They do not take into account dependent demands in the leveling process. Leveling is only performed locally on a resource, sometimes leading to overloaded resources, and on-hand stocks or shortfall quantities. Because of its more limited nature, the overall result of capacity leveling is less comprehensive than constraint-based planning.

- Infinite capacity planning with capacity leveling is less automated than a system that is capacity constrained. A capacity-constrained system, because it is automated, allows for more planning reruns without the necessity of rechecking the capacity consumption.

Keeping in mind the above limitations, it is also important to remember few companies are using constraint-based planning (which is the opposite approach from capacity leveling) or - if they have implemented a constraint-based planning approach - few are using it successfully. There are many barriers to effective constraint-based planning, which are discussed in detail in the SCM Focus Press book *Supply Planning in MRP, DRP and APS Software*. Therefore, I will not get into detail here.

A description of capacity leveling and SAP is available at this link.

http://www.scmfocus.com/sapplanning/2008/05/08/capacity-leveling-in-snp/

The Bill of Material in MRP

The Bill of Material (BOM) is the most important data structure in MRP and is really at the heart of MRP. Taking the finished good and calculating all of the dependent subcomponent need dates is called "exploding the BOM." However, not many people get to see how exploding the BOM is actually done and it is something that is important to visualize in order to fully understand what occurs when MRP is run.

In the following paragraphs, I will demonstrate the BOM with a very easy-to-use supply planning application created by Demand Works, called Smoothie. Smoothie contains both demand planning and supply planning functionality, but for this demonstration I will only show tables used in supply planning. Smoothie has a file structure so simple and well laid out that it is very easy to see how the BOM is exploded, depending on a demand.

What is a BOM?

A BOM is simply a list of input items that connect in a predefined way to an output item (or items) in certain proportions and that takes a certain amount of time to be converted. For discrete manufacturing (e.g., automobiles, toys and tools), the relationship tends to be between multiple input items and a single output item. However, in process manufacturing, where the final item cannot be broken down and converted back to the original input products (i.e., cheese cannot be disassembled into its original components, but an automobile can), one input item can convert to multiple output items, or multiple input items can convert to multiple output items. All of these relationships can be easily modeled in a spreadsheet. While a more extensive explanation is available in the SCM Focus Press book *Supply Planning in MRP, DRP and APS Software*, the spreadsheet below demonstrates a process-industry BOM that is exploded by MRP.

from_item	to_item	link_type	offset_days	factor
BEER	ALCOHOL	0	0	0.050
WINE	ALCOHOL	0	0	0.120
LIQUOR	ALCOHOL	0	0	0.400

This is a process BOM because it has a factor, which is less than one, meaning that there is a conversion between quantities and they are a percentage. The "to_ item" is Alcohol, which is converting to the "from_ item," which is Beer, Wine and Liquor. More Alcohol is used in the production of Liquor than Beer, and this is only one of the ingredients of each of these output products. The "offset_days" is currently set to zero, but in reality, the manufacturing process takes time and should be higher than zero.

Understanding Explosion

"Explosion" essentially refers to the multiplicative calculation performed by the planning system method, in this case MRP. In the example above, if 1,000 items of liquor are demanded, then 400 units of alcohol (1,000 x 0.4) are demanded, in addition to a similar multiplication of 1,000 for any other items that are also connected to the Liquor from_item in the BOM (not shown in the simplified BOM above). Explosion could just as well be called "finished good to input product relationship multiplication." The input products to the BOM are the dependent demand. Their demand is "dependent" upon the demand of the finished good.

MRP's Impact on Purchasing and Manufacturing

MRP is a purchasing and material conversion (by "material conversion" I mean "production") scheduling system. It has two main functions:

1. MRP batches the production orders and creates the necessary purchase orders at the right time so that material can be brought into the factory on time to support the production schedule.

MRP for Manufacturing Items

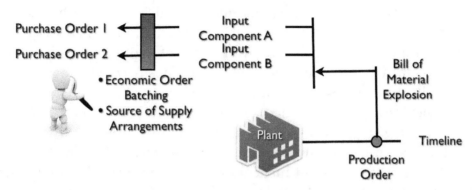

2. For procured items, MRP converts sales orders into purchase orders at the right time so that material can be brought in on time to support the sales orders. Additionally, the purchase orders are batched to meet order minimums and to create economic order quantities.

MRP for Procured Items

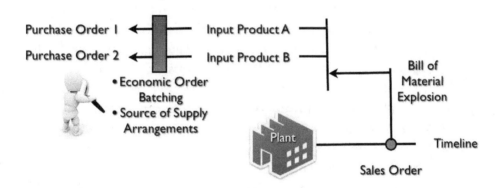

In this way, both MRP for procured items and MRP for manufactured items are inbound methods.

The Master Production Schedule

The master production schedule (MPS) is one particular application for MRP functionality. And MRP is just one way of performing an MPS. MRP is typically run in either full MRP mode or MPS mode.

The MPS is a curious entity. It is how the demand flows to supply planning. As pointed out by the book Factory Physics it "..provides the quantity and the due dates for all parts that have independent demand." As stated by the book Orlicky's Material Requirements Planning 3rd Edition, "The MPS expresses the overall plan of production. It is stated in terms of end items, which may be either shippable products or highest-level assemblies from which these products are eventually built in various configurations according to a final assembly schedule. The MRP system "believes" the MPS, and the validity of its output is always relative to the contents of that schedule." The MPS is normally a specific planning run in the supply planning application. The MPS is confusing because it has several different incarnations. When it is in the supply planning system, it is relatively easy to understand. However, as pointed out by Smith and Ptak,

> *"On occasion it has been suggested that the MPS, that is, its preparation and maintenance, could be automated and brought under complete computer control. This is envisioned as an extension of the process of automating systems and procedures in the area of manufacturing logistics. Where statistical forecasting of demand applies, so the reasoning goes, the automated forecasting procedures could be integrated into a program of MPS calculation, including preparation of the schedule of factory requirements, netting product lot sizing and so on. The logic of the procedures can be clearly defined, and all the required data are available. This notion must be repudiated. All the required data are, as a matter of fact, not available. Information on a multitude of extraneous factors, current company policy, and seasoned managerial judgment - all of them bearing on the contents of an MPS - cannot be captured by the system. This is why management should be involved in the creation and maintenance of the MPS every step of the way."*

What this means is that when companies have been calling their system run MPS, without extracting it and interacting with it, they have been not performing their MPS properly.

The term "MPS" is a bit of a misnomer, as the word "master" in MPS makes it sound as if it is a comprehensive plan. In fact the opposite is true, as MPS is a subset of the overall product database. Master actually refers to the procedure applying to the most important, or the most critical, products. Upon reflection, MPS could be more accurately described as the "critical material planning procedure," as it is used to identify critical products such as those that are constrained or have a high profit margin. Therefore, the word "master" refers to the importance of the materials modeled in the MPS rather than the **comprehensiveness** of the MPS.

When a planning run that includes all products is called an "MPS," the term is not being used correctly. A more accurate description for a planning run of this type is the "initial planning run," or the "network planning run." MPS is a particular way of running a supply planning (and initial production planning) method. The MPS is not in fact itself a method.

SAP users may find the term "MPS" especially confusing; see this post which describes how SAP has named MPS in SAP ERP.

> http://www.scmfocus.com/sapplanning/2011/06/18/why-mps-is-misnamed-in-sap-erp/

The focus on critical materials is not unique to the MPS. One common design has critical materials planned in the APS system, while non-critical materials are only planned with MRP. MPS can use the MRP functionality to come to its recommendations; however, MPS does not have to use MRP. As a result, when an APS system is implemented, the MPS process often moves to the APS system, but may no longer be called MPS. Essentially, an MPS becomes a planning run in which critical products are given priority access to all of the capacity before other less-critical items are run through. Alternatively, the MPS can simply be the main planning run that may be performed in the APS system, leaving non-critical products to be processed with MRP.

Performing the MPS in APS Systems

The following question might naturally arise: why is an MPS necessary when using an advanced planning system and when the differentiation between critical and non-critical materials has already been made (with critical materials planned by SCM and non-critical materials planned by MRP)? The answer is that there are a number of ways to get to similar results. When an APS system is included in the solution design, the MPS process most often moves to the APS system. However, APS systems have far more flexibility in terms of how the methods within APS produce the MPS. Most prominently, two of the methods within APS systems can constrain the MPS, so that the MPS becomes feasible. When this is performed, MPS can be accomplished without capacity leveling. Systematic (as opposed to manual) capacity leveling is only necessary when the plan is not using constrained resources. For instance, SAP APS's module SAP SNP (Supply Network Planning) has the ability to constrain supply resources (such as truck capacity resources) as well as production planning resources, while SAP's Production Planning and Detailed Scheduling module (PP/DS) has the ability to constrain production resources. However, constraining supply capacity in the supply planning process is far less common than constraining the production process. (PP/DS can constrain and plan in more detail on production resources than can SNP).

The Importance of the Planning Time Horizon

In addition to running the critical items prior to the less-critical items, the planning time horizon determines how **far forward** in the MPS run the critical items are able to consume capacity. This is an important, but sometimes overlooked, feature of the planning time horizon. By pushing the MPS planning time horizon out further than the MRP runs, greater priority is given to the MPS items, which is what most companies tend to desire.

Conclusion

MRP was the first computerized supply planning method to be developed. MRP is simple, but was an important first step at reducing much of the busy work involved with supply planning. DRP and, to a lesser degree, supply planning heuristics, are related to MRP. While MRP is concerned with the inbound movement of material into a location for the purposes of production, DRP is concerned with the flows of material between locations and supply planning heuristics can be used both for the initial plan and for deployment. MRP can be used to create an MPS when it is performed for only critical materials. Although MRP and MPS are terms that are frequently used interchangeably in industry, MPS is a particular way of running the initial supply plan and is independent from MRP as a supply planning method. MRP is not capacity constrained and creates an infinite and thus infeasible plan. This means that the results of MRP cannot ordinarily **all** be met by the company or by the company's suppliers. To make MRP results realistic, both material and resource limitations are introduced with capacity leveling. This, however, is only one of MRP's limitations; there are several limitations related to MRP and DRP that are primarily related to their simplified assumptions. These limitations motivated the development of APS software for supply planning.

By analyzing a spreadsheet that shows the BOM, MRP logic can be understood, except for the consumption planning logic that batches the MRP order recommendations. BOM's describe the relationship between input materials and output materials, the numerical relationship between input and output, and the time required to perform the transformation. There are other factors that are important to MRP, such as the consumption logic settings, which batch the resulting orders; however, the BOM is the heart of MRP. That is why the BOM is foundational to understanding MRP.

CHAPTER 6

Net Requirements and Pegging in MRP

"Net requirements" is simply a method of comparing and calculating the overall planned supply to overall planned demand for a product at a location. It is the primary calculation which is performed within any MRP system and as the book *Factory Physics* points out, one of the five things that MRP does along with lot sizing, time phasing, BOM explosion and iteration (repeating these steps). The following quotation is helpful with regards to net requirements.

> *Net requirements calculation is carried out in MRP in the planning run after the planning file check at the plant level. The system checks whether it is possible to cover requirements with plant stock and fixed receipts already planned.*
>
> – SAP Help

Net requirements from this description can be said to be exactly what the name implies, a **comparison of supply to demand**. Net requirements is calculated for not only MRP, but reorder point planning as well. When net requirements planning is triggered tells you a lot about the procedure.[1] In reorder point planning, the net requirements calculation is only carried out once the stock level has fallen below the reorder level. It is calculated as follows:

Plant Stock + Receipts (PO's, firmed planned orders, firmed purchase requisitions) = Available Stock

– SAP Help

Net requirements is triggered for MRP planned products whenever MRP is run. Now let us compare this to net requirements in MRP. The basis for forecast based planning is the forecast of the total requirements.

Plant Stock - Safety Stock + Receipts (POs, firmed planned orders) + Requirements Quantity (forecast requirements) = Available Stock

– SAP Help

Looking at the differences between these formulae is straightforward enough and is highlighted in blue. Here is what is different between the two:

- Safety Stock

- Firmed Purchase Requisitions

- Forecast Requirements

"At an abstract level, supply chains consist of product-location nodes, which are connected by links. That is precisely the way that Smoothie visualizes supply chains. A unique planning item in Smoothie is a node, which is connected by links. Link relationships can be factored (if one product produces a requirement for 2 of another, for example),

---

[1] This is called a replenishment trigger. Replenishment triggers, and how their requirements strategies changed per product location/combination per the manufacturing environment (i.e. make to order, make to stock, assemble to order, engineered to order), are covered in detail in the SCM Focus Press book *Requirements Strategies: Configuring Supply Planning Systems for Make to Order, Make to Stock, Engineered to Order and Planning with Final Assembly.*

and they can be offset with a lag, allowing for the possibility that nodes can be separated from one another by a significant amount of time."

"MRP models are used to represent the conversion of one material's requirement into a requirement for other materials. For example, the manufacture of a food product produces dependent requirements for packaging and ingredients. Another example might be a machine, which is assembled from many parts or sub-components (which can consist of parts...). The most complex models tend to be MRP models. They can span multiple levels, and they often involve conversion of goods using factors as multiples. The example below shows an MRP relationship that might be appropriate for the manufacture of hand tools. Notice that it includes multiple levels in depth, where a kit comes from components, and those components can be made up from raw materials. Notice also that some materials, such as the extrusions and handles, can receive demand from multiple items. Lastly, note that the screw drivers require various lengths of the same steel casting. For example, it takes 25 short screw drivers to consume a 10 ft. length of steel, so the conversion is equal to 1/25, or 0.04."

– Demand Works Smoothie Help, Version 7.3, 2013

from_part	to_part	link_type	offset_days	factor
AUTO MECHANIC TOOL KIT	SCREW DRIVER SET	0	7	1.000
AUTO MECHANIC TOOL KIT	WRENCH SET	0	7	1.000
SCREW DRIVER SET	SMALL PHILLIPS SCREW DRIVER	0	7	1.000
SCREW DRIVER SET	SMALL FLAT HEAD SCREW DRIVER	0	7	1.000
SCREW DRIVER SET	MEDIUM PHILLIPS SCREW DRIVER	0	7	1.000

SCREW DRIVER SET	MEDIUM FLAT HEAD SCREW DRIVER	0	7	1.000
WRENCH SET	1/2-INCH WRENCH	0	7	1.000
WRENCH SET	1/4-INCH WRENCH	0	7	1.000
WRENCH SET	3/8-INCH WRENCH	0	7	1.000
SMALL PHILLIPS SCREW DRIVER	SCREW DRIVER HANDLE	0	7	1.000
SMALL FLAT HEAD SCREW DRIVER	SCREW DRIVER HANDLE	0	7	1.000
MEDIUM PHILLIPS SCREW DRIVER	SCREW DRIVER HANDLE	0	7	1.000
MEDIUM FLAT HEAD SCREW DRIVER	SCREW DRIVER HANDLE	0	7	1.000
SMALL PHILLIPS SCREW DRIVER	RAW SHAFT EXTRUSION - 10 FT	0	7	0.040
SMALL FLAT HEAD SCREW DRIVER	RAW SHAFT EXTRUSION - 10 FT	0	7	0.040
MEDIUM PHILLIPS SCREW DRIVER	RAW SHAFT EXTRUSION - 10 FT	0	7	0.067
MEDIUM FLAT HEAD SCREW DRIVER	RAW SHAFT EXTRUSION - 10 FT	0	7	0.067

Pegging

Pegging is a specific and traceable connection created between a supply and a demand element. Therefore a sales order is pegged or connected to a specific production order. Pegging is an important functionality for both quality checking and creating transparency for what is actually happening the system. Pegging allows a planner to trace the set of demand and supply connections between different echelons within the supply network, including the initial demand (sales order or forecast), all of the stock transport requisitions, and all of the planned (production) orders and the purchase requisitions.

The Supply Network Flow

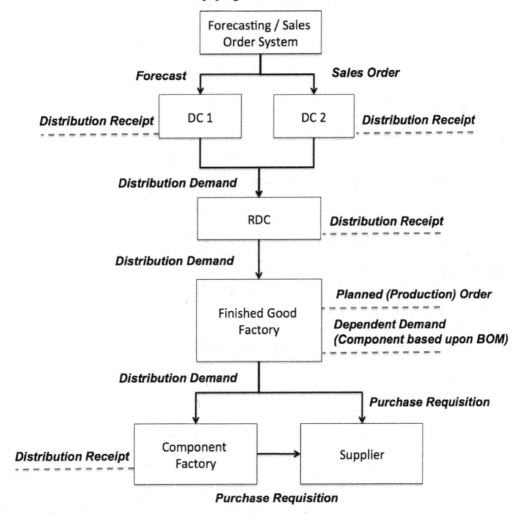

This shows the flow of requirements through a simple supply network. Pegging can help follow this flow.

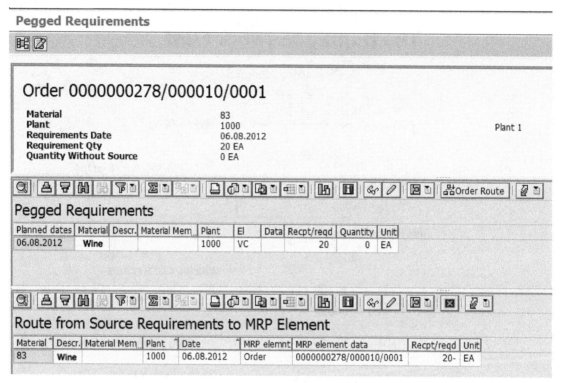

Selecting a line item and then selecting the pegging button at the bottom of the Stock Requirements List can arrive at the peggings.

Locations in ERP used by MRP

MRP operates over a series of locations within the system. As an example, in SAP ERP the following location types apply:

1. *Distribution Center:* Distribution centers (DC's) are stock-holding locations in the supply network. Companies have different types of DC's. They often have larger regional distribution centers (RCD's), which are fed by manufacturing locations and which then feed what they call DC's -normally the layer prior to the customer. (This is of course a generalization. There are many different possible supply network designs. For instance, some companies only distribute and do manufacturing).

2. *Production Plant:* Production plants manufacture product and store stock. Planned (production) orders are created by MRP in the factories, that are eventually converted to production orders.

3. *Customers:* Customer locations are of course the final destination of all products. The fact that customers are set up as locations is a bit inconsistent. Normally vendors are not set up as locations, and neither customer locations nor suppliers are considered part of the internal supply network. Whenever a location that is not inside the supply network is modeled as a location, more work results in the form of increased master data setup and additional maintenance. But it also means more visibility into that location.

4. *Vendor/Supplier Locations:* Vendors can be modeled as locations, but this is not a requirement. However, APO will have little information about vendors that are not modeled. Vendors can be set up as locations when the company wants to do the following:

The connections between the locations determine which locations can interact with which other locations.

Conclusion

Net requirements is simply a method of comparing and calculating the overall planned supply to overall planned demand for a product at a location. Net requirements and pegging provide the calculation as well as the detailed connection between demand and supply in MRP systems. Net requirements is calculated for not only MRP, but reorder point planning as well.

Pegging is a specific and traceable connection created between a supply and a demand element. Therefore a sales order is pegged or connected to a specific production order. Pegging is an important functionality for both quality checking and creating transparency for what is actually happening in the system. The ability to peg a demand element to a specific supply element is a major area of functionality of any supply planning system.

CHAPTER 7

When MRP is Applicable

MRP is often described as a universal need for companies with a supply chain, but this is not actually the case. In this chapter we will cover when MRP should be used, and when other approaches are more appropriate and will lead to better outcomes.

An Approach That Becomes Dominant

For the past several decades, MRP/DRP and ERP have become dominant concepts and dominant application categories or functionalities (as stand-alone MRP/DRP systems are not rare, its more accurate to describe MRP/DRP as functionalities than as systems). The general thinking on these topics has most commonly been the following:

1. All companies must acquire and implement ERP systems. A good example of this mindset is found in a white paper written by Aberdeen titled *To ERP or Not to ERP: In Manufacturing, It Isn't Even a Question.* This paper did not analyze any of the previous research on ERP, but simply reviewed the opinions of manufacturers, which favored the continued implementation of ERP. While not necessarily true or well researched, it is a good example of the common thinking out in industry.

2. All companies must maintain a full BOM and explode this BOM using MRP or using other supply planning/production planning methods to accomplish the same objective. This is normally proposed even for companies that outsource their manufacturing.

However, is this always the case? For companies **that perform their own production**, some type of supply and production planning system – be it MRP or MRP substitute - is a necessity. The last few decades have shown the rise of companies that design, but do not manufacture, their own products. This is in fact the common approach among high-tech OEM's. So let us first review what MRP does.

1. *Explode the Bill of Materials*: Automates the calculation of input products (raw material and components) which are necessary for a certain quantity of desired output products (finished goods).

2. *Inventory Netting*: Reduces the forecast + sales orders by the planned on-hand from the planned inventory position.

3. *Inventory Planning*: Calculates reorder points, safety stock, etc.

4. *Purchase Order Creation*: In the quantities and in the adjusted for the lead-time required to meet the demand date.

5. *Production Order Creation*: In the quantities and in the adjusted for the lead-time required to meet the demand date.

6. *Create Stock Transfers:* This is technically not part of MRP, but is the output of DRP - however, when people refer to "MRP systems" they are actually referring to both MRP/DRP, as they work in conjunction. A system with only an MRP procedure would have no way of creating stock transfers and moving stock through the supply network.

Now let us review how these MRP/DRP functions are used or not used by companies that outsource their manufacturing:

1. *Explode the Bill of Materials*: **No**

2. *Inventory Netting*: **Yes**

3. *Inventory Planning*: **Yes**

4. *Purchase Order Creation*: **Yes** - but only at the finished good level.

5. *Production Order Creation*: **No**

6. *Create Stock Transfers:* **Yes**

Therefore, even companies that outsource all of their manufacturing still need to use an MRP or other supply planning system. There are other ways to perform these same activities - and all the more advanced supply planning/initial production planning methods provide the same categories of output - however, this book is about sticking to the simpler side of the supply and production planning continuum and so MRP/DRP is still useful.

Do Companies that Outsource Need to Have a Manufacturing BOM in Their Supply Planning System?

I want to be careful to be specific here so as not to cause confusion.

1. *Is the Topic of Discussion the Design BOM or Manufacturing BOM?* There are many different types of BOM's, however for our purposes here we only need to be concerned with the design BOM and the manufacturing BOM (or MBOM). The design BOM is, as the name implies, the BOM that is produced by the engineering and design side of the business.

2. *Must the OEM (original equipment manufacturer) Instantiate and Maintain an MBOM in their MRP (or other supply planning/production planning) System? :* There is no doubt the OEM **will have a design BOM**. It is their design after all. However, the question is – if they do not perform any manufacturing, do they need to maintain the MBOM? The answers is no, because the OEM does not need to explode the BOM because they are not communicating with their suppliers detail below the finished good. This is because the CM (contract manufacturer) is delivering the finished good to the OEM.[1]

---

[1] A contract manufacturer is the outsourced manufacturing entity to the OEM. OEM's are typically the brand name entity that markets and distributes the product. GM, Toyota and Apple are all examples of OEM's. In a normal customer-supplier relationship, the product is handed off between the companies. But in contract manufacturing, the subcontractor in effect becomes a part of the company and, from concept through to

The Alternative Design 1: MRP at Finished Good Level at OEM

Instead, the OEM can move directly from the forecast for the finished good and then send the finished goods forecast – which is actually the same as the OEM procurement plan - to their contract manufacturer. The steps in this process look like the following:

Limited Planning Model for OEMs

Step	Action	In Which Entity?	From Which Entity?	To Which Entity?
1	MBOM is Sent to **CM**		OEM	CM
2	MBOM is Setup in **CM** MRP System	CM		
3	Finished Goods Forecast is Created	OEM		
4	MRP is Run at **just the** Finished Goods Level	OEM		
5	**OEM** Finished Goods Supply Plan is Created	OEM		
6	**OEM** Supply Plan is Sent to **CM** with POs		OEM	CM
7	**CM** Runs MRP and Explodes the BOM	CM		

This design can be used with a product called Arena Demand. Arena Solutions, a PLM/PDS vendor, has a product called *Arena Demand* that can allow the OEM supply plan to be aggregated and then exported to a file to be sent to the CM. It would allow the following to be performed.

- The demand report is intended for general quoting.

- From a top-level demand plan, the OEM probably would use a spread-sheet and type in the fields themselves.

---

manufacturing, the process requires collaborative input from both the customer and the supplier as if they were one company. Contract manufacturing essentially changes the OEM into more of a general contractor, with the work being performed by the subcontractors. Contract manufacturing is its own detailed topic with its own subject matter experts who are specialists in such things as how to choose the best contract manufacturer (CM) under all possible circumstances. The CM is not simply selling a product to its customer, but is offering an outsourced manufacturing capacity. The company buying from the CM has a great deal of flexibility in terms of defining the specification that is then manufactured, which also implies a great deal of information sharing, much more than is necessary for a normal supplier relationship.

- As the CM already has the BOM in their MRP system, they would be able to derive the component demand themselves.

- The OEM can't see the component demand (if they don't run MRP) and therefore Arena Demand enables them to see the component demand based on the supply plan.

- The OEM is able to use this information to quote component cost across the market to ensure that each component is taking advantage of the purchase volume planned for the upcoming months.

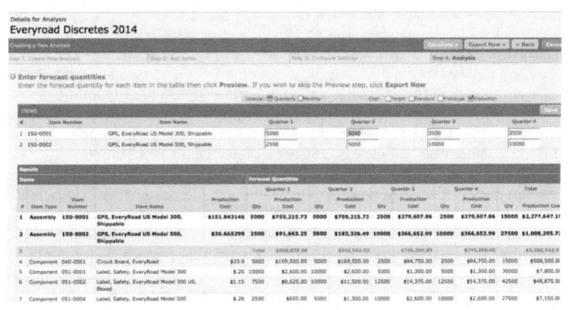

Notice the quarterly supply plan shown above for the two GPS units. This is a finished goods supply plan and, because there is no BOM, there is no necessity for the Arena application to calculate lead times – that calculating is performed by MRP when the CM has provided feedback to the OEM on the feasibility of the OEM supply plan, and when PO's have been sent from the OEM to the CM. Notice that in the upper right corner there is an export button, which is used to export the supply plan to a file. Also notice that this is just one possible planning bucket – one can also choose the monthly planning bucket rather than quarterly. Arena refers to this as the "Interval."

The Benefits of the Alternative Design

The OEM gets a much easier and lower cost to maintain system, and the complex manufacturing is moved to where it should reside at the CM, as they are actually planning the production. Some companies attempt to actively plan their CM/subcontract suppliers; however, while this may work when the OEM is a sizable part of the demand of the CM/subcontractor (and there are still complications in this – a detailed explanation of the type of software than can relatively easily handle this requirement is covered in the SCM Focus Press book *SuperPlant: Creating a Nimble Manufacturing Enterprise with Adaptive Planning Software*), if one represents only a small fraction of the demand of a CM/subcontractor capacity, it makes little sense to model this plant – in fact it is highly unlikely the CM/subcontractor would be willing to share capacity information – it's simply not worth their time.

The Relationship Between MRP and Forecastability

MRP is a forecast-based planning system. It assumes a certain level of forecast accuracy, which in turn assumes a certain level of forecastability on the part of the product/location combinations. I have analyzed a good number of product databases over the years, and many of the products that I have analyzed from different companies are clearly unforecastable. There is a simple reason for this. Many products that are difficult to forecast have no discernible pattern in their demand history and, without a discernible pattern, no mathematical algorithm can create a good forecast. For statistical forecasting, the only products that can be forecasted are those that have a discernible pattern to their demand history, and not all products have this pattern. Forecastability can usually be determined - or at least indicated -without any math by simply observing a line graph of a product's three-year demand history. If there is no discernible pattern, it is unlikely that the product is forecastable with mathematical methods. (Products that are using just the last few periods to create a forecast are the exception to this rule.) An algorithm that can appear to be predictive can be built for unforecastable products, but more often than not this is an illusion created by the forecaster who over-fitted the forecast.

Products that have a very stable history exist at the other end of the continuum of forecast difficulty. Typically, it is very easy to forecast for products with a stable demand history; however, if this is the case, actively forecasting the product does not add very much value to supply planning (the ultimate consumer of the demand plan) because a product with stable demand history does not need to be forecasted. Products with stable demand can be managed effectively and efficiently with reorder point logic, where orders are based upon a reorder point or a reorder period.

Intermittent - or "lumpy" - demand is one of the most common features of a product's demand history that makes a product unforecastable. Services parts are the best-known example of a product with lumpy demand. However, I have come across intermittent demand in many different types of companies. For instance, one of my clients was a textbook publisher. A large percentage of their product database had an intermittent demand history, which would normally not be expected of this type of product. However, due to the fact that different US states buy textbooks in large volumes whenever funding comes through, the demand ends up being quite unpredictable for many books. A school system will not make any purchase for some time, and then will buy many textbooks all at once. For example, California is on a seven-year procurement cycle, which means that they wait seven years between purchases.

Trends in Lumpiness Case Study 1: Trader Joe's Versus Normal Supermarkets

Across different industries, lumpy or erratic demand histories are becoming more common. ToolsGroup has also observed this phenomenon and wrote about it in their white paper, *"Mastering Lumpy Demand"*. One reason for the increased prevalence of lumpy demand histories is that the number of products that must be planned keeps increasing. This would not be a problem if the growth in the number of products matched the growth in demand, but it doesn't; the number of products easily outpaces the growth in demand. This is referred to as "product proliferation", and is driven by the introduction of new products without the removal of low volume items from the product database. Product proliferation is described in many articles and research papers, although strangely the phenomenon is not usually tied back to forecasting. Product proliferation reduces forecastability, meaning, of course, that the company must carry more inventory. The increased costs imposed on the supply chain because of product proliferation are generally not estimated.

The increased number of SKU's maintained by companies can be used to quantify product proliferation. Simply comparing pictures of older grocery stores to present day supermarkets can also make it obvious. Today's supermarkets are so much larger and so filled with variety, that they would be unrecognizable to people from previous eras. According to the Food Marketing Institute, present-day supermarkets carry between 15,000 and 60,000 SKU's, with the average being around 45,000.[2] Trader Joe's, still in operation today, is representative of grocery stores that maintained fewer SKU's in the past. Trader Joe's is a specialty food retailer (they can't really be called a supermarket) and they carry approximately 4,000 SKU's per store. Unlike supermarkets that have a high number of low-turning SKU's, Trader Joe's eliminates poor selling items. This strategy allows them to have a sales per square foot figure that is twice that of Whole Foods, another very successful grocery chain, and places them in a much better position from a forecasting and overall supply chain planning perspective. With fewer SKU's and fewer lower-turning SKU's as a percentage of the database, Trader Joe's is in a better position to have a lower forecast error and therefore more efficient management of their inventory than would a typical supermarket. This also translates into a lower cost supply chain.

Many strategy consultants and software salesmen like to tell their clients that any complexity added to the supply chain can be managed with advanced tools and advanced techniques. This is incorrect and most of the people making these claims do not know enough about supply chain management or software to make these proposals. Part of a supply chain's efficiency and resulting costs is a function of the discipline that is employed to limit the number of products. One step in this direction is to reduce product proliferation. However, Trader Joe's rational approach to SKU management is an anomaly; the fact is, product proliferation is likely here to stay.

Examples of Unforecastable Demand

The central premise of this chapter is that many products are inherently unforecastable. As was stated earlier, a lack of forecastability can be determined mathematically and it can also be determined visually. I find that displaying the graphics of unforecastable products is a very educational exercise, and I

---

[2] Something that is not frequently discussed is that this proliferation is only possible because products are now shipped from such vast distances, meaning grocery items can be produced in one location and shipped thousands of miles away. The average produce in a supermarket travels 1,500 miles between the farm and the retail location.

have used this technique with clients to get the point across. A visual representation of unforecastability is better, in my view, than representing the same thing with a series of numbers in columns.

The following graphics are examples of unforecastable demand history. An analysis of each is provided below the screen shot.

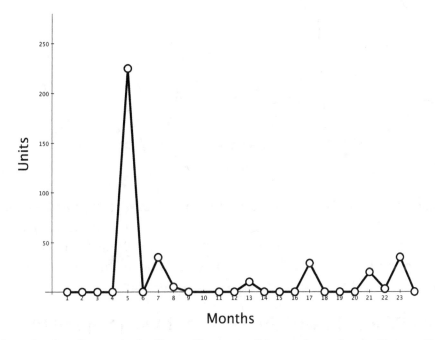

This product is clearly statistically unforecastable as there is no discernible pattern. This product has one demand peak in month seven (July), and several other smaller demand points, but simply not enough to forecast another demand point. This is a fairly obvious unforecastable demand pattern. The next example is a bit more complicated.

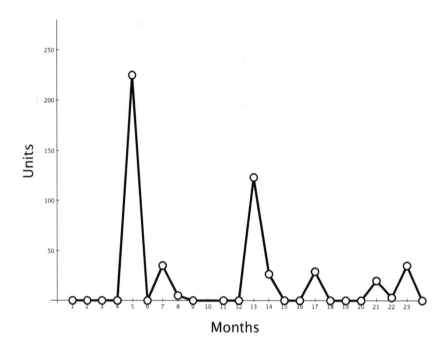

Months

In this case there are two demand peaks, and it might appear to be a good bet that the demand peak will repeat a third time...except it is not a good bet, because the first peak is in month five (May) of the first year, and the second peak is in month one (January) in the second year. Where this product is going next is anyone's guess. This product is also unforecastable.

Managing Products with No Forecast with Supply Planning

One might think that it's not really possible to simply stop forecasting products. In fact, it is quite possible and easy to implement, although there can be a fair amount of complexity in the methods designed to calculate reorder points (something that is not commonly understood by those that oppose reorder point planning on the grounds that it is too simple). In the book, *Supply Planning with MRP/DRP and APS Software*, I cover reorder point planning differently than it is covered in a number of supply planning books, so I won't repeat the information here. Suffice it to say that there are many cases where it is better not to send a forecast to the supply planning system, and the supply planning system will still manage quite well. Therefore, a simple moving average forecast can be sent for unforecastable products or no forecast at all.

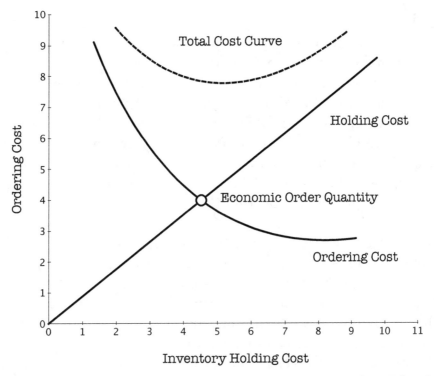

Reorder point setting does not require a forecast because the order is placed when the inventory drops to a certain level. However, there is not "one right way" of doing this. Regardless, the company gets away from continuing to invest effort in forecasting unforecastable products.

Analyzing the forecastability of the product database is one of the important steps to moving toward a more effective way of managing the forecasting process. For some products, a more advanced forecasting method cannot reasonably be expected to be an improvement over a simple, long duration moving average forecast. A number of trends are reducing forecastability of the product database, including actions by marketing (such as promotions) and SKU proliferation (spreading the same demand over more products). Interestingly, the connection is not frequently made between these trends and forecastability. The more erratic demand becomes, the less forecasting can add value, and increased amounts of inventory must be carried to ensure that sufficient inventory exists when demand does arrive. This fact is lost on people who are unfamiliar with forecasting.

Conclusion

The presentation of MRP to executive decision makers has been overly simpli-fied – often in order to facilitate the sale of software. MRP or other supply plan-ning system is required for companies that perform internal manufacturing, however this is not the case for companies that outsource their manufactur-ing. For those companies, an alternate and far less effort approach to supply planning is to simply send the demand plan to their contract manufacturer. In outsourced manufacturing environments, the two companies must collaborate on and share the bill of materials, but the company performing the manufac-turing typically will want to control MRP.

Secondly, in order for MRP to work well, the forecast for any particular item must be of a reasonable level. However, many products do not meet this qual-ification. Sometimes this is due to the skill level, training, system, etc. on the part of the company. However, other times it is due to the nature of the de-mand history itself for a particular product. Forecastability can usually be de-termined - or at least indicated - without any math by simply observing a line graph of a product's three-year demand history. If there is no discernible pat-tern, it is unlikely that the product is forecastable with mathematical methods. Intermittent - or "lumpy" - demand is one of the most common features of a product's demand history that makes a product unforecastable. Unfortunately, as is covered in the SCM Focus Press book *Promotion Forecasting: Techniques of Forecast Adjustment in Software*, a number of factors are combining to re-duce the forecastability of product databases. This includes factors such as the increase in the number of SKU's carried – called product proliferation, reduced product lifecycles and higher turnover, and increases in promotions. The less forecastable the product database, the less that an MRP, or any other supply planning method, can do to provide a good supply plan. With Sales and Mar-keting running strategy at most companies, companies are making it increas-ingly difficult on themselves to have a manageable supply chain. It also means that some maintenance areas must be performed with increased frequency on the MRP system. This is a good segue into our next topic, which is how to im-prove MRP systems.

CHAPTER 8

Specific Steps for Improving MRP

MRP implementations have common areas where they can be improved. I have run into quite a few companies that were unhappy with their MRP systems. But on the other hand I rarely run into many companies that put enough into their MRP systems. One of the great misunderstandings in this area is that migrating to a new system with a new more advanced supply and production planning method (i.e. cost optimization, prioritization, etc.) will solve the issue of MRP dissatisfaction. Most companies that think this way have not properly maintained their MRP systems, so they don't actually know what they could get out of them. The evidence that I have seen is that companies that have a problem maintaining MRP systems have **even a greater problem** maintaining more advanced methods. The reason for this is that MRP systems have comparatively less maintenance and are easier to understand and troubleshoot than the more complex methods within advanced supply planning systems. For instance, compared with other supply and production planning methods, such as prioritization or cost optimization, MRP is far easier to understand. There is also an enormous processing time difference between MRP and, say, cost optimization or cost optimization. I have performed a planning run for a supply network, which took 3.5 hours with a prioritization/allocation method. However, the same planning run took 10 minutes with MRP. That extra processing time is due to extra calculations that are required to account for the extra complexity. One example of this is how MRP breaks down the planning problem. This is called decomposition. Every supply planning method - from the least advanced MRP/DRP to the most advanced inventory optimization and multi-echelon planning - has a sub-problem and sequence that controls the processing and therefore sets the upward boundary on the interdependence between locations that can be exercised by the system. The older methods of supply planning, such as MRP, DRP and heuristics, have little interdependence between locations. For instance, MRP is only concerned with bringing in material to a location and creating production orders. MRP can be run for any product location or indeed for all products at one location without upsetting the overall plan – which is why planners often rerun MRP right from within the MRP systems' user interface – the same thing cannot be done with other supply planning methods because the decomposition of the problem is far more complex, and rerunning the procedure for one part of the problem, without doing so for the rest of the problems, upsets the planning output.

Secondly, the more advanced methods all use some of the same data as MRP systems. So lead times, inventory parameters, sales orders, forecasts, the bill of materials or the recipe are all the same. The areas which are different include the user interface, the calculation method and the way that the problem is calculated. More advanced methods also tend to have more functionality and more complexity in areas such as pegging. For instance, MRP can only perform dynamic pegging (that is the pegging changes per planning run); however some advanced planning systems can perform fixed pegging, so once an association between a demand element and a supply element is created, it will not change on the next MRP planning run. Another difference is constraint-based planning - more advanced supply planning methods can constrain resources, while MRP cannot. However, getting back to what the systems have in common, issues with lead times, inventory parameters, sales orders, forecasts or the bill of materials or recipe should be resolved or at least improved within the MRP system before moving to a more advanced system. Contrary to what many think, there is no waste in doing this because after the inputs are improved within MRP, they are simply ported to the new supply planning system whenever it comes online. Therefore whether improving the MRP system to continue to use the MRP system, or improving the MRP system in preparation for migrating to a more sophisticated supply and production planning method, I have found the following to be consistent areas of opportunity.

MRP System Comparison

A major problem with the MRP systems used by companies is that they have no means of comparing the MRP planning output to another system. This is a problem because it makes diagnosing the system far more difficult. Companies can run their live or production MRP system in simulation mode – which is where a separate copy of the data is created, but the same hardware is used to process the procedure – and the simulation results do not actually impact the live version. The benefits of this are explained in the following quotation:

> *"In the demo version of the system you can try and work out what the limits of your system are. If you have a question and you can configure your system to accept the change you can test it. If the test goes wrong when you operate the system then you will know how the system reacts and can avoid doing that on the real system. From doing this experiment you can gain insight into how you can further improve the system."*
>
> – Making MRP Work: A Practical Guide to Improving Your System's Performance

However, I am proposing going a step beyond simply creating a simulation version and testing every change in one MRP system. For a number of years now, I have advised clients to stop thinking in terms of a single solution for supply planning and to entertain more than one supply planning solution-including external simulation tools and general optimization solvers - that can enhance their company's capabilities and meet more requirements that any one tool can, even with expensive enhancements. Doing this is an uphill battle because the large consulting companies promote the mindset that all of the supply planning needs of a company can, and should, be met by a single application model. Financial incentives blind large consulting companies to better ways of doing things. And while this is the official position of the large consulting companies, it is also the position of IT that wants as few applications to maintain as possible.[1] In most cases, MRP is run from an ERP system. The problem with this is that ERP systems are in most cases difficult to diagnose and troubleshoot. ERP systems excel at enforcing an enormous number of rigid rules and processes on a business. This has positive and negative consequences, although the ERP vendors and the major consulting companies tend to emphasize the positive consequences if for no other reason that they make money selling and implementing these systems. In some cases, vendors and consulting companies will discuss the "best practices", but in many cases what is offered in the software is simply a generic practice, or specifically a logical sequence. It is a logical sequence that one would post a goods issue prior to a goods movement, and very difficult to see how this is innovative, requires special thought or constitutes a best practice. In fact, many countries have accounting rules that state this must occur in this sequence. There are also many cases where a generic practice is to create the forecast before creating a supply order, at least for a make-to stock-environment. There is nothing particularly intelligent or insightful about this sequence, it is just how it should naturally be performed. This is a natural sequence in the same way that opening a car door should precede starting the car. One can instead choose to start the car by rolling down the window, starting the car from outside and then opening the door to get in, but it would make little sense to follow this alternative sequence. Therefore, ERP systems in my estimation did not do anything to enable MRP to be run better than it had prior to ERP systems – although this was promised to be the case because ERP systems were so integrated. Integration does not improve the actual functionality, and most ERP vendors stopped developing their MRP functionality years ago – building it to an elementary state, and then choosing to focus on other things.

Therefore, most ERP systems are not the best systems in which to troubleshoot and diagnose MRP problems. What can be effective is to run MRP for just a small number of products and review and document the results, make a change to the system, and then rerun MRP and re-review and document the results. However, changing inventory parameters in many ERP systems is often

---

[1] However, even a single application can have too much maintenance if the application is naturally higher in maintenance.

a tedious process. However, there are smaller and nimbler MRP systems that can be purchased to allow a person to run MRP much more quickly; then the output from this external system can be used to check the results within the ERP system. Some of these applications are inexpensive and, in my experience, the improvement in efficiency easily makes up for the costs of the software. I believe this so strongly that I purchased this software myself for my consulting practice, as many companies prefer to not buy an MRP application for a month or two of analysis – and this allows me to use an MRP application, which can literally run circles around any ERP-based MRP functionality.

Set and Respect the MRP Frozen Period

Pretty much every company I have consulted with had issues differentiating between planning and execution. In fact, the knowledge level of planning is generally not high in companies – even companies that have invested significantly into a planning system. Planning systems have various planning horizons which declare not only how far out the plan will be generated but when the plan can be changed. This is because of dependencies.

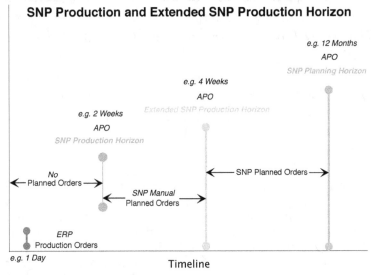

Planning systems are filled with horizons. These horizons must be integrated between the applications and essentially determine how control is passed between the systems, in addition to controlling many more aspects of the planning.[2]

---

[2] It is important to work out planning horizons as early in the process as possible. As I

The concept of a frozen period is that changes are prevented from being made when it causes a significant negative externality on some other outcome. Why have a frozen period? The reason is explained well by this quotation from PlanetTogether - a best-of-breed production planning and scheduling vendor.

Introducing too much volatility into the schedule in the short-term creates "nervousness" on the shop floor, causing inefficiencies and confusion later in the schedule.

Of course, there are also material implications to changing the production schedule at the last minute, in that the semi-finished and component materials may not have sufficient lead-time to supply the changed production schedule. The frozen period is described quite accurately by the book *Factory Physics* in the following way:

> "Since early planned order releases are the ones in which change is
> most disruptive, a frozen zone, an initial number of periods in the
> MPS in which changes are not permitted, can drastically reduce the
> problems caused by nervousness. In some companies the first X weeks
> of the MPS are considered frozen. However, in most real systems
> the term frozen may be too strong, since changes are resisted but
> not strictly forbidden. The earliest time fence, say for 4 weeks out is
> absolutely frozen – no changes can be made. The next fence, maybe 5
> to 7 weeks out is restricted by less rigid."

---

look back on the many hours spent researching this topic, I can say I have never been satisfied with the documentation that has been available to me. I have gradually come to the realization that timing settings in planning systems are a topic worthy of much more emphasis both in terms of documentation, as well as time spent on projects, than they typically receive. Because planning horizons, calendars and time settings are difficult to conceptualize until one actually sees a system where the timings have been entered, experienced consultants most often push the timing-related discussions until the demo or proof-of-concept stage of the project, allowing the client to see how these factors influence the planning output and to make their changes after this process. This is why I wrote the SCM Focus Press book *Planning Horizons, Calendars and Timings in SAP APO*. This book covers all of these timing-related topics in an integrated fashion. It is most valuable for those implementing SAP APO. However, it would be helpful for any person on a planning implementation who is attempting to figure out the integrated system timings.

Many people, particular those from Sales and Marketing, believe that the only objective of a company is meeting customer demand. This is not true. Customer demand must be met in a profitable manner, and this means a certain level of efficiency, which in turn requires a certain level of planning and stability. Much of the reason for short-term changes to the plan within what should ordinarily be the frozen period is because of incorrect inventory management policies. Inventory, not "manufacturing flexibility," is in most cases supposed to be the buffer against demand and supply variability.

This brings up the topic of supply versus demand driven supply chains. The currently proposed thinking is that all supply chains must be demand driven. In manufacturing, forecasting tends to be very highly patterned on companies that take a demand sided approach to balancing supply and demand. In this environment, the company more or less responds to demand. It creates a forecast, then measures its forecast, as well as each type of forecast (statistical, sales, etc..) against the actual sales to determine its forecast accuracy, and then creates production schedule which allows production orders to be moved forwards or backwards in order to meet this demand. That is the standard approach, and it is codified in demand, supply and production planning software to work this way. However, not all companies operate from this set of assumptions. Some companies have strong abilities to do the following:

1. *To Shape Demand:* That is to control the mix of products that are consumed by its customers through incentives or education (when education is what causes a switch in demand, this is often a complex product) and or are in less competitive markets and able to sell most of what they produce regardless of whether it matches exactly what customers want. This last point is an interesting one, as the ability to do this lies on a continuum. Extreme examples of this include defense contractors, and a notable example being the Abrams tank produced by General Dynamics that through political lobbying has been able to forced upon the US Government to purchase tanks that the Pentagon has repeatedly declared it does not need and cannot use. (although government contracts are make to order, and not forecasted in any case). Another example is the F-22, a fighter plane which most objective specialists in the area consider to do nothing well (those that defend the F-22 tend to be on Lockheed's

payroll in one shape or form) and have to have no reason to continue to be purchased, but which is still purchased due to the "demand shaping" of political donations on the part of Lockheed Martin. (Lockheed Martin maintains 1000 permanent lobbyists in D.C.) However, there are less devious examples of companies that have a strong control over demand simply based upon their market position.

2. To Substitute Demand: Some companies, due to the nature of their products, can alter products at the point of customer purchase. Paint is a good example of this. At Home Depot, starting with white paint and adding a dye in the store can create many colored paints. This converts the environment to one where many demands can be met from the same input stock – and where customization is postponed until right before the purchase. The company may prefer to cover much of the demand from a color mixed at the factory, but stocking out does not lead to a lost sale because of the onsite mixing ability at the retailer.

Some of these companies do not actually produce a demand forecast, but instead may use a few demand side inputs to skip the actual demand forecast and jump right to the production schedule. That is the company measures the accuracy of what it actually produces versus what it planned to produce.

Lead Time Accuracy

In order for the MRP system to provide correctly timed planned production orders and purchase requisitions, lead times need to be as accurate as they can be reasonably made to be. This includes not only the lead times on procurement duration and production duration, but also the offset of the lead times – which is the "lag" between manufacturing. This lag is set on the BOM or recipe in the ERP/MRP system. The example below is from SAP ERP.

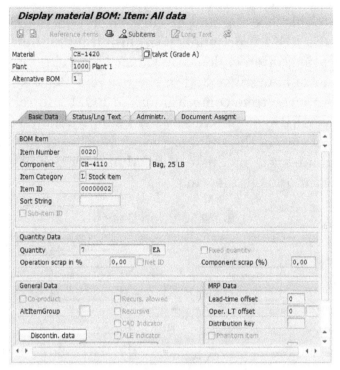

Notice, in the lower right hand corner, the field Lead Time Offset.

The objective here should be to tell the planning system the "truth." Comments about reducing lead times should be subordinated to what the lead times actually are. As soon as the lead times actually decline, this master data can be updated.

BOM or Recipe Accuracy

The BOM or recipe is the relationship between the finished good and all input products. Obviously any inaccuracy with respect to the BOM will result in anything from the wrong input products being procured to the wrong number of units being procured. All MRP systems should be considered passive recipients of BOM and recipe information and never the "system of record" of this information.[3] The place to maintain the original copies of the BOM or recipe

---

[3] When a master data object is shared among multiple applications, it is important to declare which system is the system of record. The system of record is the authoritative source of information. When a system is identified as the system of record for a master

and to perform troubleshooting and quality control on the BOM is not in the MRP system as the BOM functionality is quite limited, but within a specialized BOM application, often called a "product life cycle" or "PLM system." A very small number of hours invested in the use of a BOM system can provide better results than large time commitments to BOM and recipe improvement through using the MRP system. Those with a supply chain background tend to have a very limited view of the BOM or recipe. Neither the BOM nor the recipe begin in supply chain systems, instead BOM and recipes begin their life with product development and engineering.

BOM Solution Design

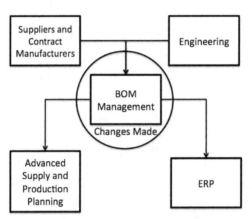

Here is a broader view of how the BOM or recipe flows through the company's applications.

---

data object, this means that (ideally) all changes should be made in the system of record and then fed to the "child" systems. The system of record can be a table or a spreadsheet. Whichever system of record is used, it should be capable of managing the master data object for which it is assigned. It also must be comprehensive, meaning that the system of record must store the full complement of fields that make up the master data object. The problem with BOM management historically is that systems chosen as the system of record for the BOM have met neither of these criteria. Historically, spreadsheets have been the most common system of record, although many companies do not have one system of record for the BOM. Instead, different groups that are responsible for the operation of various systems maintain different information about the BOM in different systems, resulting in data inconsistencies, visibility issues and archival issues. The BOM is then disjointed and its ability to be managed and leveraged for future products is compromised.

Low BOM management productivity is a major problem at the majority of companies that use BOM's. This chapter has described several reasons for this problem. One is that ERP systems set a low standard for BOM management, and this standard has since become accepted as how things are done. Most executives have never seen a demonstration of BOM management software and, furthermore, they are being told by the large vendors and consulting companies that the BOM's can be effectively managed in a disjointed fashion, or that they should focus on expensive and poorly-defined PLM solutions. These PLM solutions distract from the most important and needed functionality: to effectively manage a large number of BOM's.

I can show this easily by simply comparing a leading BOM/PLM solution to a leading ERP/MRP solution with respect to the BOM and recipe screens.

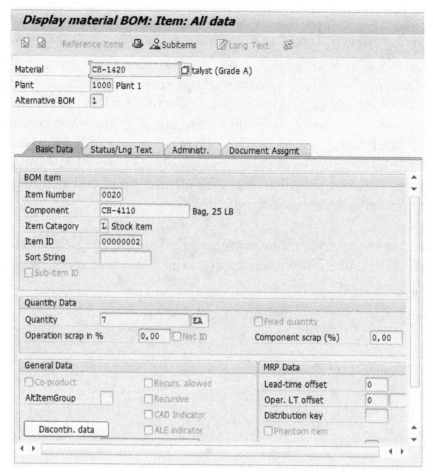

This is the first screen of the BOM for a particular product in SAP ERP. Notice how basic the data is on this screen.

Display material BOM: Item: All data

🔲 🔲 | Reference items 🖶 👤 Subitems 📝 Long Text ⥮

Material	CH-1420	talyst (Grade A)
Plant	1000	Plant 1
Alternative BOM	1	

Basic Data | Status/Lng Text | Administr. | Document Assgmt

BOM Item

Item Number	0020	
Component	CH-4110	Bag, 25 LB
Item Category	L	Stock item
Item ID	00000002	

Item Text

Line 1	
Line 2	

Item Status

☐ Engineering/design
☑ Production relevant
☐ Plant maintenance
Spare part indicator ☐
Relevant to sales ☐
CostingRelevncy [X]

Further Data

Mat. Provision Ind. ☐
☐ Bulk Material
☐ Bulk Mat.Ind.Mat.Mst
Prod. stor. location ☐
Prodn Supply Area ☐

Here is the second screen. Most of these fields simply deal with how MRP will deal with this product, for instance whether the BOM is relevant for Sales, whether it is relevant for costing.

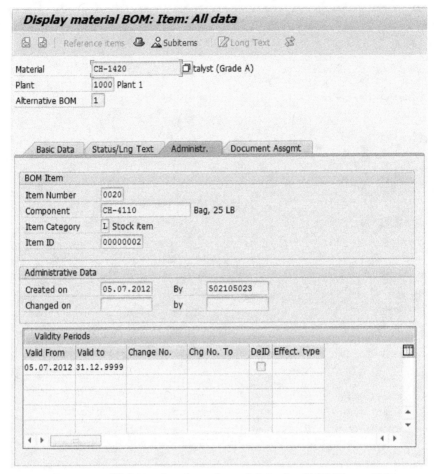

Here is the second screen. This is the date for which the BOM is valid.

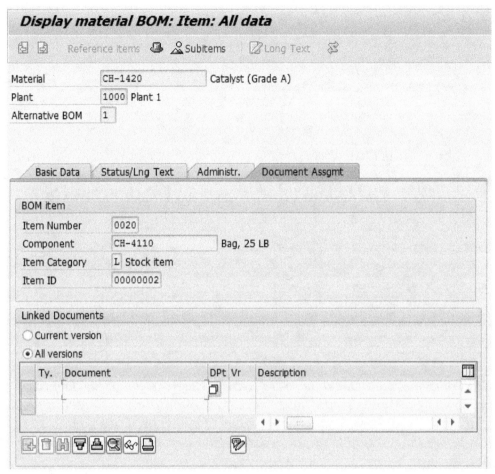

Here documents can be added to the BOM.

As should be clear, this does not provide very much visibility to the BOM or recipe. It is not a good environment for troubleshooting or quality checking BOM's or recipes. Now we will look at a specialized BOM management application.

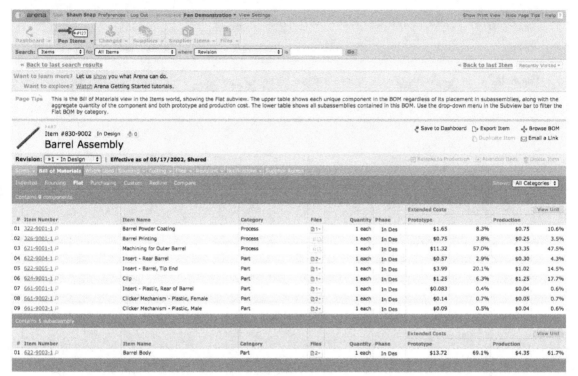

In Arena Solutions, the BOM shows very clearly. Here is a list of all the products that are part of this BOM along with their price, their quantities, their category, etc. This is the flat view of the BOM. There is no display of which products go into which other products before they go into the final product. However, that is easy to change just by changing the view.

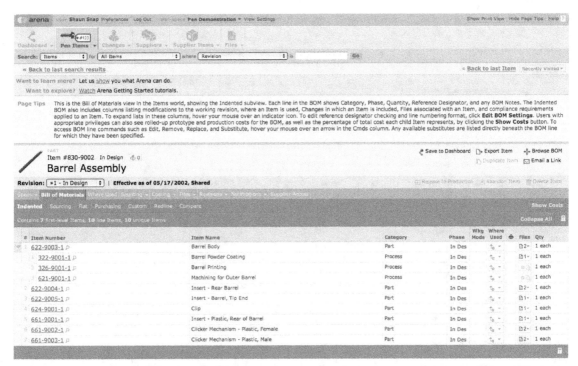

This is the same BOM, but from within a different view within the application. Now one can see that the Barrel Powder Coating, the Barrel Printing and the Machining for the Outer Barrel are children of the Barrel Body product/part. In fact, the indented BOM, as can be seen, not only shows products/parts that are children of other products/parts, but the manufacturing process step as well.

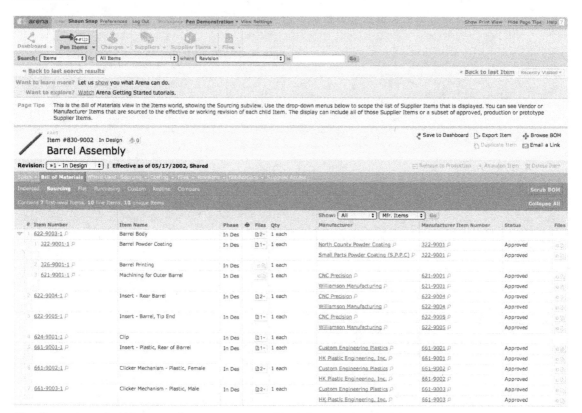

By changing the view again we can see all of the product/parts as well as their current status.

I could go on an on with the superiority of a dedicated BOM or recipe management application in terms of improving BOM quality, but this is covered in detail in the SCM Focus Press book *The Bill of Materials in Excel, ERP, Planning and PLM/BMMS Software*. For those that require further evidence and have a real interest in fully understanding how to leverage technology to improve BOM management, I recommend this book. The synopsis is that most companies are using poor applications to manage the BOM, and they pay a heavy price in terms of both productivity and BOM quality. BOM's can be managed in specialized applications, that are available at a low monthly cost (most often through SaaS delivery) that can completely change how the BOM is managed for the better.[4]

---

[4] For those that work in process industry manufacturing, you would need a recipe man-

Capacity Information Accuracy

MRP is an unconstrained method of performing supply and production planning. This is why MRP is called a "two step procedure", because a second capacity leveling step is required. This capacity leveling moves planned production orders either forwards or backwards. This capacity leveling can be performed either by a procedure or manually – or by some combination of the two. Capacity information declares how much various resources can be loaded. The lower the accuracy of the capacity information, the more that two types of errors will be made – either shifting production to time buckets and resources where capacity is insufficient, or shifting production away from time buckets and resources where there is sufficient capacity but where the resources states that there is insufficient capacity.

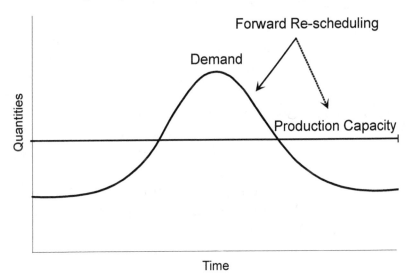

*Forward rescheduling means the company will carry more inventory as it is produced **ahead** of the need date. This is counterintuitive to the graphic because it appears as if the demand or planning production order is being moved "backwards." However the forward rescheduling refers to the relationship between the availability of the inventory versus the demand.*

---

agement, not a BOM management application – like Arena Solutions that I have showcased above. One quite good recipe management application is offered by Hamilton Grant and is covered in the SCM Focus Press book *Process Industry Manufacturing Software: ERP, Planning, Process Control, Recipe Management & MES Software.* http://www.scmfocus.com/scmfocuspress/production-books/process-industry-planning/

However, this is often considered to the alternative, which is forward scheduling, which means the order will be late versus the need date.

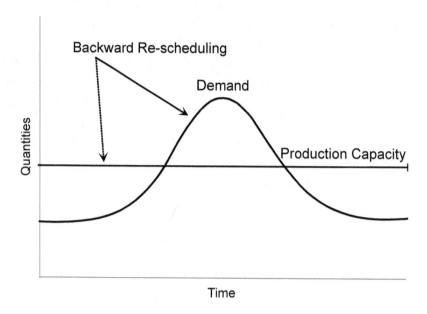

Planners often work with Sales to determine which customers can be postponed and which cannot. However, the more accurate the capacity information, the more what is communicated to customers is right – which has a strong impact on customer service.

Of course many companies do not perform capacity leveling in MRP. This is because the ability to see the interactions from the capacity leveling in almost all MRP systems is not high. This is expressed in the following quotation.

> *"Many businesses use an external capacity tool to help with their planning. The most common method I have seen with this is via a spreadsheet. Whilst the more visual element of the spreadsheet can help people come to grips with the information contained in the system it can also cause problems if the tool falls into the "workarounds" category...The issue I witness most often is the capacity planning spreadsheet has the current capacity information held within it whilst the MRP has obsolete data (with respect to capacity information). This situation can lead to accurate top-level schedules being scuppered (to sink or destroy) by work to lists that*

don't reflect the requirements of the business. It is no wonder how
some businesses can get their manufacturing teams so confused."
     - Making MRP Work: A Practical Guide to Improving Your
     System's Performance

Companies are in a bit of a bind with respect to maintaining capacity information in MRP. Officially, one should maintain as accurate as possible capacity information in the MRP system; however, MRP systems don't provide much capacity leveling visibility in order to perform capacity leveling effectively. Some of this depends upon the particular MRP system in question.

Assignment to Forecast-based or Consumption-based Planning

Many companies use MRP to plan products with a high forecast error and then are disappointed with the results. However, MRP, as well as other supply and production planning methods, requires some" level of forecast accuracy. Forecast inaccuracy can be driven by factors that are related to the quality of the forecasting process (which can be changed) and factors inherent to the product/location combination (which often cannot). The common refrain within companies is that "if only our forecasts were better…"; however in the short-term, the forecast accuracy is what it is. The role of supply planning is to deal with this forecast accuracy – whatever it may be. MRP is a forecast-based planning method. Without sufficient forecast accuracy, MRP cannot do much for you.

Many companies think that there is no clear way to determine which product/location combinations should be placed on MRP (also called forecast-based planning) versus reorder point or consumption-based planning. However, a consistent and intelligent calculation can be used to make this segmentation. I sometimes use a forecastability formula in order to determine which product/location combinations should be place on MRP planning and which product/location combinations should be placed on consumption or reorder point planning (this is also sometimes referred to as "Lean".) This sets a definitive threshold of which product/location combinations will be planned in the way that is most appropriate for them. This should be performed for the entire product/location database, and the setting changed accordingly in the MRP system. Once forecast accuracy improves for the high error product/location combinations, they can easily be switched to MRP-based planning.

Inventory Parameters

The history of computerized supply and production planning going back to the early 1960's has been an example of increased sophistication of the method being employed. Some of the mathematics behind these methods is quite impressive, however the problem is that there has been little change and in fact little focus on parameters (with the exception of safety stock, which is both over-emphasized and confuses most companies in terms of calculation) that maintain a powerful control over the planning output. This has reduced the value that these systems have been able to provide to the companies that purchased them. This is just as much of a problem in the most advanced systems as when MRP systems first began to be used back in the 1970's.

Every method in supply and production planning, including of course MRP, interacts with inventory parameters - they are the control fields that you provide the model with important assumptions. For instance, if an order is received for 100 units, without parameters, in most cases a production order for 100 cases would be scheduled. It is a parameter that tells the system that because of costs, a minimum production order is 500 units – therefore to meet this demand a production order of no less than 500 units should be scheduled. A few of these better known parameters include the following. The inventory parameter master data I would like to discuss is the following:

1. *Safety Stock*: The stock carried specifically to account for demand and supply variability. Many companies use rules of thumb to set safety stock – such as using two weeks of demand. These rules of thumb are imprecise. A rule of thumb of two weeks of demand does not account for variability of demand or variability of supply. Many applications have dynamic safety stock functionality. However, in most cases, companies back away from using dynamic safety stock as set up in these applications. This leads to the next point.

2. *Service Level*: When dynamic safety stock is used, it means entering a service level in the product master per product/location combination. I have yet to see this approach of leveraging the dynamic safety stock func-

tionality within either MRP systems or many other types of advanced planning systems actually work – even though consultants frequently recommend it, many of whom have never personally tested the dynamic safety stock formula. Using the dynamic safety stock functionality already within MRP systems sounds like a good idea but, in fact, it is an unnecessarily simplistic way of setting safety stock because the safety stock set this way is not integrated to the other inventory parameters for the particular production/location combination, or to the safety stock other product/location combinations.[5] Safety stock should be determined per particular service levels. Given limited resources, giving a very high service level assignment to one product location means necessarily taking it from others. Service levels can be determined at the finished good level for make-to-stock environments or at the raw material and component level for assemble-to-order environments. It can be determined at the product/location combination only, or for a grouping or products. Even where some of the service levels are partially overridden, the company still comes out with a comprehensive and consistent set of service levels that are embedded in supply and production planning parameters.

3. *Procurement Min Lot Size:* The minimum procurement lot size. Procurement lot size is often a trade-off between inventory carrying costs and ordering costs.

4. *Production Batch Size:* The minimum produce lot size.[6] The production batch size is a trade-off between the costs between production runs both in the form of changeover costs (cleaning, machine adjustment, etc.) and inventory carrying cost and inventory space considerations.

---

[5] More on this topic can be found at these links: http://www.scmfocus.com/supplyplanning/2014/04/08/safety-stock-calculator/http://www.scmfocus.com/sapplanning/2012/04/08/the-issues-with-the-use-of-dynamic-safety-stock/ and http://www.scmfocus.com/supplyplanning/2014/04/08/safety-stock-calculator/, as well as the SCM Focus Press book *Safety Stock and Service Levels: A New Approach.*

[6] A company can meet different service levels with either inventory or more flexible manufacturing – that is they can choose where to incur the costs and the costs between inventory and manufacturing flexibility are inversely related. Therefore, the application should help them decide what is the correct trade off between the two costs. Lot sizing applies equally for manufacturing as well as for inventory planning.

5. *Reorder Point:* The stock level at which the company should re-order. All supply and some production planning systems have reorder point planning. All that is required to use this functionality is to identify the product/location combinations that should be placed onto reorder point planning (something that we can do -- although part of a separate forecasting analysis), assign the calculated reorder points and associated parameters. The final step is to activate reorder point planning as the method that controls the product/location combination in the system. Reorder point planning is a low maintenance way of managing portions of the product/location database - and frees the planning team to spend more time on other combinations.

It is an illusion that safety stock or service level, or these other values above, are set appropriately during an implementation. I have found that in many cases these values are still improperly set years after the implementation is live. Interestingly, most of the effort by software vendors in this area has been in developing more complex methods. This is done to increase the sell-ability of software, but does not improve the **implement-ability** of the software. In fact in most cases, the more complex the method, the less implementable is the software, but the higher the potential improvement that exists.

Giving the Business the Parameter Support it Requires to Plan Properly

On implementations, both software vendors and consulting companies generally assume that these values are all known by the client, and that all that remains is to simply take these values and populate the new system. However, the reality is that, for the most part, the business sides of companies do not have effective ways of setting these parameters. Just because the parameters pre-exist in an already-implemented system **does not mean** they are anywhere close to acceptable values.

The issue is a matter of specialization. Business resources within companies must manage a system, but are not expert at inventory management and parameter setting, and do not have the opportunity to study the topic and apply parameter changes to multiple companies. Setting the parameters essentially requires a research project where the individual product locations are analyzed, inventory formulations are customized for the specific requirements and needs of the company, and - this point is sorely missed by companies - the parameters are set within the context of the overall product location database so that a usable policy is created. Planning departments are simply not staffed to perform this type of research. In fact, it is far less cost-effective to try to hire this knowledge in-house because the parameters do not need to be, and in fact should not be, changed except periodically.

Calculating the Values

All of these values can be calculated in an integrated fashion. Companies can expect to see improvements in planning outcomes - less inventory, better service levels - **within a few weeks** after the project is complete. In terms of cost-to-benefit ratio, no software implementation or business consulting improvement project in the area of inventory management can compete with this type of parameter calculation project. This is because of the combination of the short duration along with its highly usable and extremely likely improvement in the inventory parameters, which directly results in a better plan. Finally, out of this process, the company learns what its service levels should be – which provides a major benefit not only to Supply Chain but to Sales as well. These service levels could be adjusted by Sales, but the calculated service levels provide a great baseline and understanding of what a profitable service level is for a particular product, and Sales typically appreciates the guidance.

An Inventory Parameter Calculation Project

I want to be very clear that the company should not look at this as software that they must purchase. It also does not mean replacing the main supply planning system – rather this process helps the currently installed supply planning application by tuning it – by providing it with the input that it requires to provide the best output.

Important details of these types of projects are the following:
- *Universally Applicable Output:* The calculator is used to process the records, which your IT group can then upload to the supply planning system. The output works for **any** ERP system and **any** advanced planning system.
- *No Software to Purchase:* Because there is no software to buy, there is little pushback from IT. An inventory parameter calculation project tunes

the existing system with no other investment other than the time to develop the calculator.

- *Combined Approach:* Safety stock and service level should be calculated in conjunction with one another, and in a way that is cognizant of the safety stock of other product location combinations..

- *Customization:* Each safety stock/service level improvement project leverages the standard calculator, but adjustments can be made depending upon what you want to accomplish.

- *Semi-Permanent or Periodic Review:* Putting this effort and intelligence into setting the service level and the safety stock means that the company has an even greater incentive to reduce manual approximations and overriding the safety stock values. Once set, the safety stock should not be adjusted, however as time passes the calculations should be updated with the more recent information. This keeps the safety stock values up to date – and the normal terminology that describes this is a "periodic review". This is no different from the other inventory management parameters such as minimum lot size.

As should be clear, I have given a great deal of thought and performed a great deal of research into this topic. I have developed a calculator to everything that I have listed in this subsection which can be used to improve any MRP system. This calculator is explained in Appendix B: Inventory Parameter Calculation with 3S.

Determining the State of an MRP Implementation

Before beginning an MRP improvement project, it is important to understand the usage level of the MRP system. It's not sufficient to ask executives this question, as they receive most of their information about the system second-hand and are not in the system dealing with its output. However, an understanding can typically be determined from just a few interactions with those that use the system. I have also found it important to list the statements that are collected from these interactions. This is because, when combined, the statements can be triangulated and can provide insight into the system's usage.

Company XYZ Case Study

Now that I have spent a good amount of time explaining how to perform these types of projects. Below I have a list of some of the statements made to me by one company:

1. *"Only around 12% of ERP (i.e. MRP) driven recommendations are followed.*

2. *Sales orders are often entered after the production order is complete. This is done because it is not always known what the production quantity will end up being. By entering the sales order after the production order, the sales order and production order match in quantity.*

3. *We run MRP.*

4. *We have a forecast accuracy of... (this number varies – but estimations ranged from 25% to 40% accuracy on a monthly basis measured by MAPE - mean absolute percentage error - at the product location combination).*

5. *New production orders are created and scheduled for the following week for the same item, which is still being run this week. Because the quantity that will be produced this week is still not known (as the run is not complete), the production order is not created until after the production run is complete.*

6. *Sometimes we use a forecast, but sometimes we don't and we just use the sales order quantities from the previous month.*

7. *We divide our products into short lead time and long lead time products with short lead-time products going out on MRP, and long lead time products going out on reorder points.*

8. *I am concerned with master data for this project because we have very little master data in the system, such as correct routings."*

These statements tell us quite a bit about how the system is used. Below I have listed some obvious conclusions from these statements.

1. Based upon statement 1, it's clear that the company is not really using the MRP procedure for planning. The MRP output is changed manually

so frequently that it is more accurate to describe the system as manually planned. Statement 3 points out that they run MRP, however with such a high percentage adjusted, MRP does not actually decide very much.

2. Statement 2 shows a breakdown of the normal sequence of orders. Statement 5 is another example of the same issue. The company does not even commit to its production orders one week out. This means that the production order is begun in the factory, and both the production order and sales order are created after the production run is complete. These orders are a recording step, the planning step of creating requisitions probably does not occur. The concept of an ERP system is that the system initiates the activities in real life, not that ERP simply **records** what has already occurred. If this is all true, then the purchase orders or stock transport orders must also be manually created, in order to have material for the factory to use for production. These must be created manually as the production orders are not in the system prior to the component lead times, requiring them to be placed. This further means that the planners must be manually exploding the BOM, i.e. using a spreadsheet with the BOM to calculate how much material is needed to support each production order.

3. The forecast accuracy, be it either 25 or 40%, is so low, that MRP, a forecast-based planning system, cannot add value to the process for the items with the lower forecast accuracy (this is an average, so some products probably can be planned with MRP if the master data for production details and lead time were correct). Therefore, most of the products would fall to a reorder point planning approach.

4. On statement 6, this individual was not aware that this is in fact a forecast. However, this can be setup in SAP ERP demand management. But, from his description, it sounds to be yet another manual override.

5. Statement 8, combined with many statements related to the problems with master data, tells us that the output quality of requisitions and orders of this system would have to be quite low. This is one of the major factors that has promoted the company to treat an ERP system as a recording system for decisions that they make with external support tools.

6. Further interviews with external procurement and deployment groups showed that the MRP does not drive purchase orders and that the DRP procedure's stock transport requisitions are in the vast majority of cases overwritten manually.

The synopsis of these statements is that the ERP system **was not** controlling the decision-making for supply chain planning. Instead, the ERP system is used to record what has already happened. The users of the system do not trust the system's output, and most likely with good reason. In fact, the reasons are contained within the quotations above.

All of this gets to what is the primary point of this case study. This is not a fully implemented ERP system. Instead, it is a partially implemented system but one for which some of the most important preconditions that are required for a planning implementation do not exist. Secondly, it is quite possible that many executives within the company do not understand this. That is, they think they have fully implemented ERP several years ago, and are thus prepared to implement an advanced planning system. The graphic below describes the difference between how the ERP system is actually being used, and how the executives at this company think it is being used in this case study. I performed this analysis for a company that was moving from MRP to more sophisticated planning methods in an advanced planning system, however the same approach applies to any MRP improvement project. It is necessary to determine the current usage level of the system. The following graphic explains how a company's MRP implementation can be graded on a continuum.

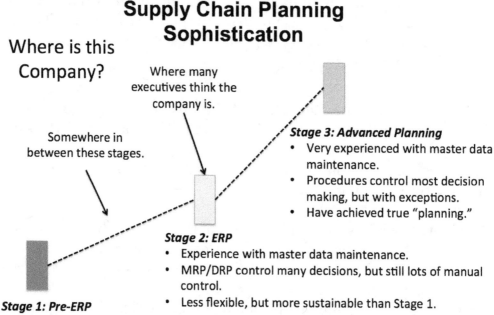

Supply Chain Planning Sophistication

Where is this Company?

Where many executives think the company is.

Somewhere in between these stages.

Stage 3: Advanced Planning
- Very experienced with master data maintenance.
- Procedures control most decision making, but with exceptions.
- Have achieved true "planning."

Stage 2: ERP
- Experience with master data maintenance.
- MRP/DRP control many decisions, but still lots of manual control.
- Less flexible, but more sustainable than Stage 1.

Stage 1: Pre-ERP
- Little experience with master data maintenance.
- Most decision made with human controlled logic.
- Tendency to not follow strict rules.
- The ultimate in flexibility.

It's important to understand the level of usage of the MRP system. The fact that a MRP system is "live" does not mean that its processes are being followed. Companies that are in some state between a pre-ERP versus a full-ERP environment do not typically successfully implement advanced planning systems. There is hierarchy of system and supply chain planning sophistication that a company must have achieved in order to successfully move to the next level. Those companies that find themselves with an impending advanced planning implementation, but which do not have a full-ERP environment implemented, must move to migrate to a full-ERP environment as quickly as possible by changing how they use the their ERP system to be in conformance with its design.

Conclusion

There are variances in terms of what are the largest areas of opportunity for improving MRP systems; however, a significant opportunity exists at every company I have encountered to make a small project focused on improving MRP worth the effort. It should be understood that any MRP improvement project should be undertaken with an open mind regarding the areas of opportunity, because in many cases the company itself is not only unaware of where the opportunities lie, but also how large the opportunities are.

An MRP system can be diagnosed and from there a prioritized list of what to focus on can be created. Typically there will be a funding limitation – even though MRP improvement projects generally don't take very long – there tends to be much less appetite for spending money on fixing an MRP system than there was for funding the initial MRP/ERP system implementation. I am not sure why this is the case, but it may have something to do with not wanting to pay for something twice. Most large consulting companies, along with vendors, make quite unrealistic promises of the improvement that will occur from implementing a new application. So implementing companies are most often led to believe that no further tuning of the system is necessary. This need to allocate money for future tuning and improvements, something that extremely few software vendors will agree to include into the total cost of ownership TCO calculation, is something that I set as a default value when calculating TCO.[7]

All of these adjustments take money and time. It typically makes sense to improve MRP for the most important (largest, most profitable products) before moving on to less critical products. Most companies have some very high volume products where improving MRP makes a big impact on the bottom line. Marketing, through product proliferation, tends to grow the product database so that most companies now have large numbers of products that it would actually be better for the company to discontinue, but Marketing will not allow it. Under optimal circumstances and unlimited funding, all product/location combinations would be analyzed for improvement, but in most cases this will not be feasible, so identifying the most important product/location combinations is typically an important first step which can reduce the overall work effort and bring it down to a manageable level that matches the available funding.

---

[7] TCO is strangely under-calculated and it is frequently proposed that neither software vendors, nor consulting companies nor analysts like Gartner, want TCO calculated. Instead it is far better to propose the importance of TCO as a general concept, but to never calculate TCO. This is explained in great detail in the SCM Focus Press book *Enterprise Software TCO: Calculating and Using Total Cost of Ownership for Decision Making*. http://www.scmfocus.com/scmfocuspress/it-decision-making-books/enterprise-software-tco/

Conclusion

MRP and DRP are two of the oldest methods of supply, production and deployment planning, but they are also by far the most commonly used. However, while MRP/DRP systems are old, it is a rare company that has mastered them. The first step to understanding MRP is to differentiate it from MRP II. The procedure that performs supply and production planning is MRP, not MRP II.

Two of the most important features of MRP are the calculation of net requirements and pegging. Net requirements is simply a method of comparing and calculating the overall planned supply to overall planned demand for a product at a location. Net requirements and pegging provide the calculation as well as the detailed connection between demand and supply in MRP systems. Net requirements is calculated for not only MRP, but reorder point planning as well.

Pegging is a specific and traceable connection created between a supply and a demand element. Therefore a sales order is pegged or connected to a specific production order.

MRP, as with any supply planning method, is not applicable in every situation. One example of this is in outsourced manufacturing. Many companies have outsourced their manufacturing but have continued to run MRP, which means that MRP is run within two different entities (the OEM and the contract manufacturer). In scenarios that are more subcontractor than contract manufacturing, that is where the OEM provides input materials to the subcontractor - in that case, running MRP within the OEM for those products is of course still necessary.

A second issue with MRP is that it is sometimes run for products that are not inherently forecastable, or which the company has made far less forecastable due to forecasting incompetence, or through activities by other parts of the company like Marketing that are intent on making the forecasting database as unforecastable as possible in order to meet their own narrow objectives. When a product is unforecastable, no supply planning procedure, with the exemption of inventory optimization and multi echelon planning can beat a simple reorder point. Many companies think that there is no clear way to determine which product/location combinations should be placed on MRP (also called forecast-based planning) versus reorder point or consumption-based planning. However, a consistent and intelligent calculation can be used to make this segmentation. I sometimes use a forecastability formula in order to determine which product/location combinations should be place on MRP planning and which product/location combinations should be placed on consumption or reorder point planning (this is also sometimes referred to as "Lean".)

The past several decades have witnessed a great increase in the supply planning and production planning methods that are generally available in software. This includes methods like allocation, cost optimization and inventory optimization. However, many companies that introduced new and more sophisticated applications were misled by both software vendors and consulting companies into thinking that their primary problem was that the procedure that they used (MRP/DRP) was too unsophisticated; that is, all that was necessary was to apply a more sophisticated procedure and the output would automatically improve. However, what was lost in the discussion was that a major reason that companies were dissatisfied with their MRP/DRP system was that they often did not understand it and did not invest enough in maintenance and training. These same problems persisted in the new software as well; in fact it was even worse as the more sophisticated methods of supply planning, while having major advantages over MRP/DRP, were even more difficult to maintain and troubleshoot than MRP/DRP. Major areas of oversight included the BOM accuracy, capacity information accuracy, lead-time accuracy, as well as the parameters that modify the procedure of MRP and DRP. Examples of these parameters include safety stock, minimum order quantities, deployment horizon, etc. There are simply ample areas where MRP and DRP can be improved, but there is very little focus on doing this and it is difficult to find consulting companies that focus on this type of improvement. A far more common approach is to find consultants and advisors who will recommend the purchase of a new software system, bringing in more complexity before the MRP/DRP system has been mastered. However, regardless of whether the plan is to replace the MRP/DRP system or to continue using it, there are not very many good reasons not to take a closer look at the MRP/DRP system to make improvements.

Calculating MRP

In order to improve the understanding of MRP in terms of its calculation, I have created the following form. I recommend using this form in order to see the MRP calculation in real time, and to make adjustments to the MRP inputs.

http://www.scmfocus.com/supplyplanning/2014/04/10/mrp-requirements-calculator/

This can be compared to a comparative method of supply planning, called reorder point planning, in the following calculator:

http://www.scmfocus.com/supplyplanning/2014/04/09/dynamic-reorder-point-calculator/

Inventory Parameter Calculation with 3S

I am such a proponent of integrated inventory parameter optimization that I have developed a software calculator that does just this.
This calculator is called the SCM Focus Service Level Scenario Setting and Parameter Optimizer or 3S for short.

The Conceptual Underpinnings of 3S

3S is based upon three overarching concepts, which derive from
having been in many company environments and considering the
reality of how supply and production planning systems are used.

1. *Inventory Calculations:* 3S calculates its parameter output
   through applying formulas that are similar to standard formulae that can be found in inventory management books, but
   have been customized to provide more usable output. Unlike
   an academic paper, all of our formulae need to work together
   – and we found improvements that allow them to work together better. This leads to the next point.

2. *Constrained Parameters and Parameter Inputs:* The standard
   calculations tend to assume that the capacity at the company
   is unlimited. In order to obtain constraints, most companies

purchase an expensive system. However, we have found there are ways of constraining parameter inputs that are more straightforward. In fact, one of the most interesting opportunities is the ability to use 3S to constrain systems that do not have constraints – and this is the vast majority of supply and production planning systems in use today.

3. *Global View:* 3S calculates individual values, but looks at the overall product location database to do so. This means that the individual settings are congruent with the big picture.

The Process

3S requires data that is available from most companies, but I have to format it to work with the 3S calculations. For instance, 3S does not calculate safety stock or several other values by using the normal forecast error and supply lead-time variability measurements. This means that I work with clients to access the input data and then I format it myself. Companies have similarities in their parameter needs, but they also have differences. We have standard calculations as part of 3S - but we also have the ability to adjust some of the calculations for specific customer requirements. I don't yet have the process down as a template and consider the customization portion to be important and something I am more comfortable assuring quality if I do it myself.

How S3 Output Is Updated

3S is **not an online** application, but is a **periodically-run** application, and therefore it is very efficient for clients to re-engage us and faster for us to run the application and then provide the output file – which can then be uploaded to the ERP system. This takes a load off of the planning function in the company.

Net Change Parameter Updating

Updating the service levels and parameters of a company does not mean processing all of the product location database again - instead I recommend selecting new products or products that have gone through a significant change, and processing those. This type of **net change** processing can happen at any time, and updating the parameters is not an onsite project but is engaged in remotely and requires far fewer hours than the initial project. A segmentation of product/location combinations during a net change parameter update might look like the following.

More on 3S can be found at the 3S website at http://www.scmfocus.com/3S. In my view, an integrated parameter calculation of this type is the fastest as well as the least expensive way to improve the output of not only MRP, but all supply planning and production planning methods currently in use.

References

Castenllina, Nick. To ERP or Not to ERP: In Manufacturing, It Isn't Even a Question, Aberdeen. 2011
http://aberdeen.com/aberdeen-library/7116/RA-enterprise-resource-planning.aspx

Demand Works Smoothie Help, Version 7.3, 2013

Hopp, J Wallace. Spearman, Mark L. Factory Physics 3rd Edtion. Waveland Press. 2011.

Johnson, Giles. Making MRP Work: A Practical Guide to Improving Your System's Performance. Smartspeed Consulting Limted. 2013.

Lingus, Richard G. The Rise and Fall or MRP. Rockford Consulting. 1991.
http://rockfordconsulting.com/the-rise-and-fall-of-mrp.htm

MRP. Accessed October 18, 2013.
http://en.wikipedia.org/wiki/Material_requirements_planning

Plossel, George. Orlicky's Material Requirement's Planning. Second Edition. McGraw Hill. 1984. (first edition 1975)

Plossl, George. Production and Inventory Control: Techniques and Principles. 2nd ed.
Prentice Hall, 1985.

Schroeder, Roger. G. Anderson, John. C. Tupy, Sharon. E. White, Edna. M. A Study of MRP Benefits and Costs Journal of Operations Management. October 1981.
http://www.sciencedirect.com/science/article/pii/0272696381900310

What is MRP (I,II) Full citation lacking, but available at this link
http://www.share-pdf.com/73ec30f31e4e41e29f089357308d2349/What%20is%20MRP.pdf

What is MRP Software. E2B Anytime. May 13 2013.
http://blog.e2banytime.com/what-is-mrp-software-material-requirements-planning-software-explained/

Wight, Oliver. The Oliver Wight Class A Checklist for Business Excellence. Sixth Edition. Oliver Wight International. 2005

Vendor Acknowledgments and Profiles

I have listed brief profiles of each vendor with screen shots included in this book below.

Profiles:

SAP
SAP does not need much of an introduction. They are the largest vendor of enterprise software applications for supply chain management. SAP has multiple products that are showcased in this book, including SAP ERP and SAP APO.

www.sap.com

Demand Works
Demand Works is a best-of-breed demand-and-supply-planning vendor that emphasizes flexible and easy-to-configure solutions. This book only focuses on the supply planning functionality within their Smoothie product, which includes MRP and DRP.

http://www.demandworks.com

Arena Solutions

Arena Solutions is a leading provider of SaaS based bill of material management software. Arena's Arena PLM product allows companies to collaborate on the bill of materials.

http://www.arenasolutions.com

Author Profile

Shaun Snapp is the founder and editor of SCM Focus. SCM Focus is one of the largest independent supply chain software analysis and educational sites on the Internet.

After working at several of the largest consulting companies and at i2 Technologies, he became an independent consultant and later started SCM Focus. He maintains a strong interest in comparative software design, and works both in SAP APO as well as with a variety of best-of-breed supply chain planning vendors. His ongoing relationships with these vendors keep him on the cutting edge of emerging technology.

Primary Sources of Information and Writing Topics
Shaun writes about topics with which he has firsthand experience. These topics range from recovering problematic implementations, to system configuration, to socializing complex software and supply chain concepts in the areas of demand planning, supply planning and production planning.

More broadly, he writes on topics supportive of these applications, which include master data parameter management, integration, analytics, simulation and bill of material management systems. He covers management aspects of enterprise software ranging from software policy to handling consulting partners on SAP projects.

Shaun writes from an implementer's perspective and as a result he focuses on how software is actually used in practice rather than its hypothetical or "pure release note capabilities." Unlike many authors in enterprise software who keep their distance from discussing the realities of software implementation, he writes both on the problems as well as the successes of his software use. This gives him a distinctive voice in the field.

Secondary Sources of Information

In addition to project experience, Shaun's interest in academic literature is a secondary source of information for his books and articles. Intrigued with the historical perspective of supply chain software, much of his writing is influenced by his readings and research into how different categories of supply chain software developed, evolved, and finally became broadly used over time.

Covering the Latest Software Developments

Shaun is focused on supply chain software selections and implementation improvement through writing and consulting, bringing companies some of the newest technologies and methods. Some of the software developments that Shaun showcases at SCM Focus and in books at SCM Focus Press have yet to reach widespread adoption.

Education

Shaun has an undergraduate degree in business from the University of Hawaii, a Master of Science in Maritime Management from the Maine Maritime Academy and a Master of Science in Business Logistics from Penn State University. He has taught both logistics and SAP software.

Software Certifications

Shaun has been trained and/or certified in products from i2 Technologies, Servigistics, ToolsGroup and SAP (SD, DP, SNP, SPP, EWM).

Contact

Shaun can be contacted at: shaunsnapp@scmfocus.com

Abbreviations

APS – Advanced Planning and Scheduling

BOM – Bill of Materials

CM – Contract Manufacturer

DRP – Distribution Requirements Planning

ERP – Enterprise Resources Planning

MRP – Material Requirements Planning

MRP II – Material Resource Planning

MPS – Master Production Scheduling

OEM – Original Equipment Manufacturer

(SAP) PP/DS – Production Planning and Detailed Scheduling

SKU – Stock Keeping Unit

S&OP – Sales and Operations Planning

TCO – Total Cost of Ownership

Links Listed in the Book by Chapter

Chapter 1:

http://www.scmfocus.com/inventoryoptimizationmultiechelon/2011/10/redeployment/

http://www.scmfocus.com/supplyplanning/2014/04/09/dynamic-reorder-point-calculator/

http://www.scmfocus.com/writing-rules/

http://www.scmfocus.com

http://www.scmfocus.com/supplyplanning

Chapter 3:

http://www.softwaredecisions.org

http://www.scmfocus.com/scmfocus/it-decision-making-books/enterprise-software-selection/

Chapter 5:

http://www.scmfocus.com/sapplanning/2011/02/04/level-of-bom-planning-in-the-snp-heuristic-and-low-level-codes/

http://www.scmfocus.com/sapplanning/2008/05/08/capacity-leveling-in-snp/

http://www.scmfocus.com/sapplanning/2008/05/08/capacity-planning-and-constraint-based-planning-for-service-parts/

http://www.scmfocus.com/sapplanning/2011/06/18/why-mps-is-misnamed-in-sap-erp/

Chapter 8:

http://www.scmfocus.com/supplyplanning/2014/04/08/safety-stock-calculator/

http://www.scmfocus.com/sapplanning/2012/04/08/the-issues-with-the-use-of-dynamic-safety-stock/

http://www.scmfocus.com/supplyplanning/2014/04/08/safety-stock-calculator/

http://www.scmfocus.com/scmfocuspress/it-decision-making-books/enterprise-software-tco/

Appendix A: Calculating MRP

http://www.scmfocus.com/supplyplanning/2014/04/10/mrp-requirements-calculator/

http://www.scmfocus.com/supplyplanning/2014/04/09/dynamic-reorder-point-calculator/

Appendix B: Inventory Parameter Calculation with 3S

http://www.scmfocus.com/3S

www.ingramcontent.com/pod-product-compliance
Lightning Source LLC
LaVergne TN
LVHW080100070326
832902LV00014B/2328